FROM THE PAGES OF

Journal of Northwest Anthropology
Volume 53, Number 1—Spring 2019

Why Don't We Write More? Essays on Writing and Publishing Anthropological Research

Edited by Darby C. Stapp, Julia G. Longenecker,
Tiffany J. Fulkerson, and Shannon Tushingham

NORTHWEST ANTHROPOLOGY

EDITORS

Darby C. Stapp
Richland, WA

Deward E. Walker, Jr.
University of Colorado

ASSOCIATE EDITORS

C. Melvin Aikens (University of Oregon), Haruo Aoki (University of California), Virginia Beavert (Yakama Nation), Don E. Dumond (University of Oregon), Don D. Fowler (University of Nevada), Rodney Frey (University of Idaho), Ronald Halfmoon (Lapwai), Tom F. S. McFeat (University of Toronto), Bruce Miller (University of British Columbia), Jay Miller (Lushootseed Research), Rudy Reimer (Simon Fraser University)

Julia G. Longenecker	Operations Manager
Alexandra Martin	Production Assistant
Heather Hansen	Production Assistant
Kara N. Powers	Editorial Assistant
Amanda Cervantes	Design

Composed by Northwest Anthropology LLC, Richland, WA; Printed by Kindle Direct Publishing.
Missing issue claim limit 18 months.

POLICY

The *Journal of Northwest Anthropology*, published semiannually by Northwest Anthropology LLC, in Richland, Washington, is a refereed journal and welcomes contributions of professional quality dealing with anthropological research in northwestern North America. Theoretical and interpretive studies and bibliographic works are preferred, although highly descriptive studies will be considered if they are theoretically significant. The primary criterion guiding selection of papers will be how much new research they can be expected to stimulate or facilitate.

SUBSCRIPTIONS

The subscription price is $50.00 U.S. per annum for individuals and small firms, $85.00 for institutional subscriptions, $30.00 for students with proof of student status, and $25.00 for all electronic subscriptions; payable in advance and online. Remittance should be made payable to Northwest Anthropology LLC. Subscriptions, manuscripts, changes of address, and all other correspondence should be addressed to:

Darby C. Stapp, Ph.D., RPA
Journal of Northwest Anthropology telephone (509) 554-0441
P.O. Box 1721 e-mail JONA@northwestanthropology.com
Richland, WA 99352-1721 website www.northwestanthropology.com

MANUSCRIPTS

Manuscripts can be submitted in an electronic file in Microsoft Word sent via e-mail to the Richland, WA office. An abstract must accompany each manuscript. Footnotes and endnotes are discouraged. Questions of reference and style can be answered by referring to the style guide found on the website or to *Journal of Northwest Anthropology*, 47(1):109–118. Other problems of style can be normally solved through reference to *The Manual of Style*, University of Chicago Press. All illustrative materials (drawings, maps, diagrams, charts, and plates) will be designated "Figures" in a single, numbered series and will not exceed 6 x 9 inches. All tabular material will be part of a separately numbered series of "Tables."

© by Northwest Anthropology LLC, 2019

Why Don't We Write More? Essays on Writing and Publishing Anthropological Research

CONTENTS

Introduction
Darby C. Stapp and Julia G. Longenecker 1

Part I 6
   Reflections on Writing
     Virginia L. Butler 8

   On Writing and Publishing
     Kenneth M. Ames 12

   Writing and Publishing Research and the Electronic Revolution
     Roy Carlson 16

   It's Writing, or Vacuuming
     Alice B. Kehoe 20

   On Writing Paleozoology, Zooarchaeology, Archaeology, and in General
     R. Lee Lyman 24

   Writing to a More Inclusive Readership
     Robert R. Mierendorf 29

   A Writing Philosophy
     Mark G. Plew 34

Part II 36
   Eschew BS and Insist on Disclosure
     Thomas F. King 38

   To Publish or Not to Publish—The Changing Nature of Archaeology
     Dennis Griffin 40

   If You Dig a Site, You Must Record in Detail *and* Write Up Results, Since Your Site Area is Now Gone Forever...
     Dale R. Croes 44

   Caveat Emptor, Anthropology is a Lifetime of Writing
     Kevin J. Lyons 50

   Some Hidden Facets of Writing Archaeology
     Madonna L. Moss 54

Writing Tensions: Voices That Help—and Those That Don't
Mark S. Warner 58

From Writing Science to Writing for the General Public
Dennis Dauble 61

Part III 64

A Commentary on Publishing
Bruce Granville Miller 66

Why Write
Jay Miller 70

Unearth and Heft
Nathaniel D. Reynolds 73

The Language of Writing
Astrida R. Blukis Onat 77

The Tin Shed: Why I Write
Rodney Frey 83

Conclusion—Writing and Publishing in Anthropology: Voices, Insights, and Disciplinary Trends
Tiffany J. Fulkerson and Shannon Tushingham 88

Introduction

Darby C. Stapp and Julia G. Longenecker

The world of publishing, especially academic-related publishing, is in a state of flux. The changes that have resulted from the advances in digital computing and communication technology have revolutionized the way we write, the way we read, the way we present our information, and the way we disseminate our information. Not surprisingly, the economics of publishing have been turned upside down. All of these factors are impacting the way that scholars—especially young scholars—write. The impact on disciplines such as anthropology, for which technical books and academic journals are very much the lifeblood, has been, and will continue to be, significant.

The *Journal of Northwest Anthropology* (*JONA*) has a vested interest in the changes that are occurring throughout the publishing industry and the impacts that will be felt in the academic and business sides of anthropology. As a regional anthropology journal, we must incorporate new technology where we can, adapt to market conditions as they shift, and provide our readers with the products they expect, be they books or journals, printed or digital. We must balance our mission to disseminate anthropological research with the need to stay economically viable. More than anything, however, we need content. Without manuscripts to publish, none of the rest of it—subscribers, journal design, publishing software, websites, etc.—matter. For this reason, we spend a considerable amount of time throughout the year talking with colleagues and staying up on developments in the field to keep a steady and diverse stream of quality manuscripts arriving in our inbox.

The collection of articles presented below is a result of one of these efforts, which started as an email discussion between one of us (DCS) and Tiffany Fulkerson and Shannon Tushingham (both *JONA* authors) at Washington State University concerning their research on gender, profession, publishing, and the peer-review process. At one point, the topic shifted to their recent suggestion for creating a new non-peer review journal for the Pacific Northwest, which they think might address some of the publishing problems that appear related to the peer review process (Fulkerson and Tushingham 2018). An additional thought Tiffany had was to devote an issue of *JONA* to the various forces that impact anthropological writing and publishing.

This idea struck a chord with us and within a week we decided to ask our *JONA* family to share their experiences and ideas about professional anthropological writing. We would ask for relatively short essays (1,000 words, plus or minus 500) about writing from a diverse group of *JONA* authors and peer reviewers and publish them in an upcoming issue of *JONA*. We would write an introductory essay and, since Tiffany had come up with the idea, she and Shannon could write a concluding essay.

But would anyone do it? To find out we composed the e-mail and then started down the *JONA* mailbox selecting individuals who we knew had published a lot or who we knew had a strong interest in the challenge of publishing anthropological research. We sent the email to twenty-five colleagues on October 26, 2018. To our surprise we had acceptances from a dozen colleagues within a few days, and by the deadline in December, we had nineteen completed essays (53% came from academic settings, 47% from applied settings; 79% are male, 21% are female; 63% are archaeologists, 26% cultural anthropologists, 11% ecologists (one terrestrial, one aquatic); 100% are white with average age of approximately 65). Collectively, this group of writers has written or co-written more than 150 books and more than 1,300 book chapters and articles in professional journals.

To help put the contributed essays in context, we provide the actual email sent to colleagues below to show exactly what was asked of each writer:

> Dear Colleague,
>
> I have been in discussion with Tiffany Fulkerson and Shannon Tushingham (WSU) about anthropological writing and publishing. While Tiffany and Shannon are focusing on issues surrounding gender and publishing (or lack thereof), part of our discussions have morphed into tangential topics: the (declining) state of anthropological writing in general, our perceptions that professionals are writing less these days, and ways we might encourage professionals to continue/begin writing (young, mid-career, retired).
>
> At one point Tiffany suggested that perhaps *JONA* could play a role in promoting anthropological writing. Julie and I have thought about that suggestion in the last few weeks and come

up with the concept of publishing a series of short essays by writers about writing. I'm writing to ask you, as someone who has published a variety of things in *JONA* and elsewhere, to write something relatively short for us, say 1,000 words (plus or minus 500 words), concerning your personal thoughts on anthropological writing. Below are some questions that might ignite some thoughts:

- what has been your writing philosophy?
- what has motivated you to write professionally?
- what challenges have you had to overcome to get published?
- what challenges do you see today in the world of anthropological publishing?
- what suggestions do you have for would-be writers?
- how can we as a profession ensure that anthropologists in the Pacific Northwest of all types and backgrounds continue to publish?

These questions are not intended to be answered in toto, but they could be. But more so, the intent is to offer some ideas and let you go with what moves you.

If interested, our suggestion is for you to let the words flow as they might. We see these essays as written in an informal style, inspirational, and of a personal nature (i.e., what you think, what you have experienced, what you would like to see). We're interested less on explaining the nature of the problem, and more on exploring potential solutions to the dearth of manuscripts being produced for both peer review and non-peer review outlets.

Please think about our request and let us know if you can participate. We would like something around December 15 so we can get it all put together for the next *JONA* in spring 2019 (v. 53, n.1).

The current plan is to include the essays along with an introduction to the set. Each essay will include a brief introduction about the writer with a summary of writing accomplishments.

If per chance we get an overabundance of responses, we can include more or perhaps continue the discussion in the next *JONA*.

Thank you for considering the request on this important topic.

Darby

As you read through the essays, you will see that they vary widely in both content and style (Table 1). Almost every essay provides anecdotes concerning the authors' writing past, professional responsibilities to write, and the challenges that writers face. Many of the essays provide suggestions to young professionals to help them hone their writing craft and get published. The essays provide insights to the past and present publishing world and the technological advancements that are stimulating change. Several authors address specific topics such as gender and Indigenous peoples.

The essays are divided into three parts. Part 1 essays were written by archaeologists and tend to be comprehensive. Part 2 essays were written by archaeologists and an aquatic ecologist, tend to be short, and focused on two or three topics. Part 3 essays were written by cultural anthropologists, an archaeologist, and a terrestrial ecologist, are longer, and explore cultures outside the academic world. Following the essays, Fulkerson and Tushingham present a conclusion, which draws on the essays and addresses the future of anthropological publishing.

We encourage you to read all of the essays and believe you will find them as interesting, insightful, and inspirational as we did. We are most thankful to the nineteen authors who took time from their busy schedules to share their thoughts on writing and publishing. Clearly, this group of prolific writers feels strongly on the need for anthropology to continue its strong tradition of documenting and sharing what we learn. We can only hope that the new generations of anthropologists will follow in their footsteps and adapt to this rapidly changing world where new technology is upending the way we communicate.

Table 1. Topics Discussed in the Nineteen Essays

Essay	1	2	3	4	5	6	7	8	9	10	11	12	13	14	15	16	17	18	19	
Author	Butler	Ames	Carlson	Kehoe	Lyman	Mierendorf	Plew	King	Griffin	Croes	Lyons	Moss	Warner	Dauble	B. Miller	J. Miller	Reynolds	Blukis Onat	Frey	Total
Anecdotes		X	X	X	X		X		X	X	X	X		X	X	X	X	X	X	15
Writing Philosophy	X		X	X		X	X	X		X	X		X		X	X	X	X	X	14
Why Publish/ Write? Motivation	X	X		X	X	X	X	X	X	X		X			X	X			X	13
Publication Obstacles/ Challenges	X	X		X	X	X		X				X	X		X	X		X		11
Publication Trends			X	X			X	X	X			X	X			X	X		X	10
What to Write		X	X	X		X			X						X	X	X	X	X	10
Writing Tips/ Suggestions	X	X			X	X		X	X		X				X			X	X	10
Publication Outlets		X	X	X			X	X				X			X	X			X	9
CRM Impacts		X	X					X	X	X										5
Indigenous Perspectives					X					X					X	X	X	X	X	7
Writing for the Public				X	X			X						X						4
Publishing, Editors, Peer-Reviews												X				X		X		3
Gender				X								X								2
Total	4	7	6	8	5	7	6	7	7	4	3	7	3	2	8	9	5	7	8	

REFERENCES CITED

Fulkerson, Tiffany J., and Shannon Tushingham
2018   Equity, Multivocality, and the Need for a Non-Peer Reviewed Journal for Pacific Northwest Archaeology. *AWA News*, 22(3):9–10.

ESSAYS ON WRITING AND PUBLISHING

Part 1

Part 1 contains the following essays:

- "Reflections on Writing" by Virginia L. Butler, professor and chair of the Department of Anthropology at Portland State University, where she has been since 1994. She is an archaeologist specializing in long-term relationships between people and animals, which she explores mainly using zooarchaeology. She earned her M.A. and Ph.D. from the University of Washington. Butler has published sixty-eight peer-reviewed articles and book chapters, as well as twenty-nine contract reports—mainly chapters and appendices to which she has contributed.
- "On Writing and Publishing" by Kenneth M. Ames, Professor Emeritus of Anthropology at Portland State University. He is an archaeologist. He received a Ph.D. in Anthropology from Washington State University in 1976. Ames has authored seventy-one peer-reviewed articles and chapters, and has written or edited five books; he has authored or contributed to thirty-three CRM reports.
- "Writing and Publishing Research and the Electronic Revolution" by Roy Carlson, founding Chair (1970) of the Department of Archaeology, and Professor Emeritus at Simon Fraser University. B.A. 1952, M.A. 1954 U. of Washington. Ph.D. U. of Arizona 1961. Field research and publications on the Northwest Coast, Plateau, Southwest, and north Africa. Carlson has published eighty articles, including chapters in books and monographs; sole-authored six books; and edited or contributed to seven multiple-authored books.
- "It's Writing, or Vacuuming" by Alice B. Kehoe, Professor of Anthropology, emeritus, Marquette University, Milwaukee, WI. Her Ph.D. 1964, from Harvard University drew upon fieldwork with a Ghost Dance religion congregation in Saskatchewan. Besides ethnographic and ethnohistorical research, she carried out archaeological fieldwork in Montana and Saskatchewan with her husband, Thomas F. Kehoe. Kehoe has written seventeen books and has coedited four.
- "On Writing Paleozoology, Zooarchaeology, Archaeology, and in General" by R. Lee Lyman, paleozoologist and archaeologist, Professor Emeritus at the University of Missouri-Columbia. He received a Ph.D.

in Anthropology in 1982 from the University of Washington. Since 1975, Lyman has published 20 books (5 as sole author, 9 as co-author, 6 as co-editor), more than 170 journal articles, and 51 book chapters. He has also authored 85 contract reports (mostly chapters in reports).

- "Writing to a More Inclusive Readership" by Robert R. Mierendorf, a career anthropologist since the 1970s, specializing in precontact period archaeology of the Pacific Northwest. Following retirement after twenty-plus years as park archaeologist at North Cascades National Park, he continues researching and writing through his private consultancy. Mierendorf has published thirty-two articles, two books, and five chapters in books.
- "A Writing Philosophy" by Mark G. Plew, Ph.D., Indiana University. He is University Distinguished Professor of Anthropology at Boise State University. His primary research interests are in hunter-gatherer archaeology of the Snake River Plain and Northeastern South America. Plew has published 253 books, monographs, and journal articles.

Reflections on Writing

Virginia L. Butler

I am pleased to have been asked to contribute to this *JONA* issue that includes essays about the importance of writing in anthropology. I think about writing a lot as a researcher and college professor. Writing is so fundamental to my scholarship, it is difficult for me to express why it is important. It's almost like breathing or eating. If you decide you want to be a scholar or "do research," you have a responsibility to share what you have learned to a broader audience. Otherwise—only *you* have the knowledge that comes from research. In another fundamental way, the act of writing crystalizes what you have learned, forcing you to logically explain your insight. Sometimes (maybe often), it exposes important flaws in your logic. Writing forces you to link various threads (initial goals, larger theory, and empirical findings) in a logical, coherent way. Writing is not an independent act after you complete laboratory or field work; it is an integral part of the research process. As you write, you are "figuring things out." Noted author Elie Wiesel captures this idea well: "I write to understand as much as to be understood."

In the text that follows, I share reflections on what motivates me to write, my general philosophy about writing, how I overcome challenges when writing, and suggest things developing writers can do to support their practice.

Motivation

Various factors motivate me to write. Since I like doing research, I feel a responsibility to share what I do as noted above. Whether it's the tax-payer that funds my research or a private foundation, I feel guilty if I do not "write something up" and get it published so it is part of the public record. Beyond guilt, I enjoy the sense of community in writing articles, building on other scholars' ideas and then thinking that someone will build on mine. Perhaps this is odd to admit, but posterity motivates me too. When I'm long gone, I like thinking that maybe someone will read something I've written and build on an idea there; and then pass on a kernel of me into the future.

Philosophy

My writing is guided by principles articulated in Strunk and White's classic, *The Elements of Style.* My 11th grade English teacher recommended this book to me, and I've had a copy ever since. Rules I draw on especially include the importance of active voice and the need to use specific, concrete language. But perhaps "rule 13," which highlights brevity, is my favorite.

> Vigorous writing is concise. A sentence should contain no unnecessary words, a paragraph no unnecessary sentences, for the same reason that a drawing should have no unnecessary lines and a machine no unnecessary parts. This requires not that the writer make all sentences short, or that he avoid all detail and treat his subjects only in outline, but that *every word tell.* (Strunk and White 1962:17; emphasis added)

As I write and then edit my own writing, I sense Strunk and White at my shoulder, whispering in my ear: "is that paragraph, sentence, phrase, or word necessary? Are these helping to *tell your story*?" If I can't answer yes, I omit the words. Many writers (including students) suggest that stripped down writing is dull. I will counter this criticism with "less is more." Writing that tries to convey ideas simply and clearly and uses active voice and active verbs, creates vibrant writing that can compel a reader to read more. To me, the best writing is active and concise, includes all the important detail, but nothing extra.

Challenges to Overcome

Writing is hard. It takes time, patience, and discipline to write. I can spend half a day on one paragraph. I can write 2,000 words and then decide most of them do not contribute to the paper I'm *really* trying to write. Some people are faster than others are at writing, so the hardship varies. But practically everyone who commits to writing knows it can be hard and lonely. So, how do researchers (or writers of any kind) overcome this very real challenge? Why do we persist in doing something that is so hard? I'm not sure how others do it, but I've become friends with "delayed gratification." I get a huge rush of satisfaction when

I complete a paper, then again when it is published. This helps me push through challenging writing times, it keeps me inside when the sun is shining outside. I keep telling myself how wonderful I'm going to feel when I'm done!

Some aspects of writing I truly enjoy, especially when I can view a writing project as a puzzle. The components of the manuscript for example, like the research context, project goals, results and implications, are pieces of the puzzle (and parts of these in turn are smaller units of the puzzle). I ask, what is the best way of arranging these puzzle pieces to tell the story in the most compelling way? When do I introduce this idea, or that line of evidence? I like moving pieces around, trying them out in different places to see what works best.

Suggestions for Developing Writers

First, I recommend that developing writers read widely—across all kinds of writing—and read a lot. Read academic books and articles and essays and fiction written for popular audiences (the *New Yorker* is one of my favorites). As you read, critically reflect on the writing, asking yourself whether the writing "is working"—driving you to read more, or not. Analyze how an author develops an argument, presents their ideas. Find time to read while you are writing. This practice will connect you with the writing process and give you a sense of community with others that are writing.

If you are getting started on a writing project, make yourself sit in front of the computer and commit to writing on a regular schedule. Do not wait for inspiration—you may wait a long time. The simple act of trying to write will generate some writing, promise. That start will then get re-written likely many times. That writing start will then join with the next piece of the project, and then the one after that. When you are "stuck" in your writing, try to figure out what is blocking you, but don't obsess over it. Maybe you need to work on another section for a while. When you return to the section in which you were stalled, you'll often have a new perspective and can find ways to power through. Be patient, keep trying. Think about how happy you're going to be when you have a finished draft.

REFERENCES CITED

Strunk, William Jr., E. B. White
1962   *The Elements of Style*. Originally by William R. Strunk, Jr., with revisions, an Introduction and a new chapter on writing by E. B. White. MacMillan Paperback Edition, New York.

On Writing and Publishing

Kenneth M. Ames

My 1981 *American Antiquity* article started its life as a seminar paper in the fall of 1969. I was encouraged to revise and publish it, which I did eleven years later. I spent those intervening years massaging, tweaking, completely revising, massaging, and tweaking some more. After all that stressing and work, when it was accepted, the editor of *American Antiquity* called to say I had to cut it by a third. I asked which third. He said, "Any third," which I did in four days over a Thanksgiving vacation. So much for eleven years of obsessing: "When in doubt, cut it out." The published version bares only a passing resemblance to the original and I am not sure it is better, and, had I gotten it out in a timely manner (say after five years of tweaking), I would have been well ahead of the "complex hunter-gatherer" curve. Of course, I did other things during that period: got my first two jobs, moved twice, started teaching and developing classes, finished my dissertation, got married, got divorced, ran survey and data recovery projects, wrote reports, wrote two papers that got rejected (one was eventually published) and published a couple of chapters. But still I tinkered.

The charge for these essays is to write about writing and issues such as why people are writing/publishing less, if indeed they are. I am not sure what "writing/publishing less" means; does it mean that people are writing less, or that the pace of journal submissions is declining? The proliferation of journals, growing stacks of CRM reports, and bulging files of archaeobureaucratic paperwork points to lots of writing. More journals may mean submissions are spread more thinly among them. And then there's writing, and then there's writing. Take CRM reports; some are excellent, contain significant data and intellectual capital, while others are stultifyingly boring, mechanical, and useless. Of course, the same can be said for journal articles/book chapters. So, by writing, do we mean putting words on paper; or good, productive writing, writing that moves the discipline forward in some fashion?

There are impediments to good writing, perhaps more than to bad writing. Good writing is hard work (for most of us); requiring time, discipline and focus. In academia, where writing is a job requirement, there actually isn't much support for it beyond lip service, at least in my experience. Faculty time is eaten up by a myriad of increasing demands; some essential (teaching, advising, research), some a waste of time (assessment). The structure of the faculty has changed. Gone are the days when most were tenured or tenure track, with the security to pursue long-term research and writing projects. Now, in many schools, a significant portion of the faculty are fixed-term or sessional faculty, contractors who teach one, two or more courses here, there, and elsewhere. Hard to write that journal article while commuting between campuses or teaching four courses per term. In CRM, there is less incentive to publish, especially after a day of cranking out reports or surveying wind turbine pads. That CRMers and agency archaeologists do publish is a testament to their professionalism and dedication to the discipline. The impediments also include fear, insecurity (I have nothing to say, I will look stupid, I can't write), a sense that there's no point (no one's ever going to read this), misplaced perfectionism, laziness, lack of professional commitment. And finally, as my personal anecdote shows, there's life.

So, why write? It is of course a professional obligation; publishing our work, making it available to our colleagues and ultimately the public, is one of the crucial things that separates us from antiquarians and worse. That is not to say we do that particularly well, but it is the ideal. Two additional aspects of that professional obligation are the quality of the work and of the writing itself. Neither well written poor work, or badly written good work are useful. What is good work? Rigorous scholarship of some kind, be it library research or a well conducted field survey. Good writing is, to my mind, simple, straightforward, and readily understandable, which is difficult to achieve, but more of that below. Other reasons to write are job requirements, ego, competition, ambition, desiring to contribute to the field, to shape the field, and combinations of these and other motives. Or, just because you want to, or because you have to; it's who you are. At this point in my life, that's why I write. I have other motives as well: ego, wanting to contribute—but writing is now a fundamental part of who I am.

But that doesn't necessarily ensure either getting writing done or producing good writing, as the anecdote that opens this essay shows. It took me 11 years to get that paper out because of insecurity hiding behind perfectionism, with continual revision as a way to avoid submission, avoiding risking rejection or criticism. As long as I held on to it, it was a good paper, maybe a great paper, most of all a safe paper.

How did I get past that? I did publish one paper before the *American Antiquity* paper. I coauthored it with Alan Marshall and we published it in *North American Archaeologist* after it was turned down by *The Journal of Anthropological Research*. At that time, *NAA* was new, and I figured it was a safe place to submit. It was, but the paper was well received. A confidence builder. But the most important step was participating in the 1985 volume *Prehistoric Hunter Gatherers, the Emergence of Cultural Complexity*, edited by T. Douglas Price and James Brown. Price is an excellent, but brutal editor. If I survived that, I could survive anything. My writing and publishing took off after that, partially because of the attention drawn by the volume, but partially by the increased confidence gained from that experience. But even with all that, I still struggle sometimes and get bogged down.

I am pressing my allotted 1,000 words, but I want finish with a few more words about good writing. American academic writing is notoriously bad, turgid, opaque, dense, but there are good archaeological writers. In my generation these include Kent Flannery, David Hurst Thomas, Brian Fagan, and Bob Kelly, among others. Good writing can be done, but I hesitate to give advice, since writing is a very personal activity. I once asked Jim Deetz, another excellent archaeological writer, what his secret was. He said he wrote one draft, and never revised. If it wasn't coming out the way he wanted, he set the piece aside and worked on something else for a while, and then went back to it when things felt right. Amazing, but not very helpful, at least for a mere mortal. My few pointers on writing well by mortals:

- Have your goal in writing the piece clearly in mind.
- Have a clear idea what you want to say and how you want to say. I try to know what I want to say, but often don't until I've written it. Leads me to:
- Pound out the rough draft. Expect it to stink. Don't revise while you're writing.
- Revise the rough draft. It may take three or four revisions, but don't hide behind the revisions, use them to move the paper/report along.

- Keep asking yourself "is this useful, how can I make it more useful."
- Ask yourself "How can I make it shorter, simpler? Can this text be a table?"
- Write in the active voice, avoid the passive voice. Never, ever write "Due to the fact that...." "Because" works well and it's four fewer words.
- Kill your babies. Go through and cut out all the prose and vocabulary you think is especially nifty. It is distracting. The paper is not about you, it's about the subject.
- Shorten it some more.
- Keep in mind, you may never be finished, but at some point you are done.

Writing and Publishing Research and the Electronic Revolution

Roy Carlson

The system of which anthropological writing and publishing is a part has changed, and is continuing to change, during my sixty-five years as an anthropological archaeologist. Anthropologists should be more aware than most people that culture and society do change in response to technological innovations, of which the most influential today is the Electronic Revolution that has brought rapidity and bargain-basement cost to the preservation and communication of research data and results. As in the earlier Bronze Age and Iron Age revolutions, the effects of the Electronic Revolution on society are far reaching as the socio-cultural system attempts to achieve equilibrium of its component parts, and all kinds of changes take place. Anthropological writing for publication is a small part of this system, but since its purpose is preservation and communication of both data and ideas, it was and is bound to take advantage of new technology that facilitates these goals, and will change accordingly.

My philosophy of professional writing is that the data recovered from survey and excavations are the most important part of archaeological research, even though the interpretations may at the time of publication have been much more interesting. This philosophy probably stems from the Boasian ideal of careful and precise collection of data as a prelude to synthesis. I look back at the first thing I ever published (with Warren Caldwell) on stone piling in the Plateau, published in the *American Anthropologist* in 1954, and realize it is still being cited today because of its substantive content. The data from another of my early publications on the Archaeology of the San Juan Islands (*American Antiquity* 1960) is still being used today in new and different cultural-historical syntheses (i.e., Terry Clark 2013 *Rewriting Marpole*). My doctoral dissertation, *White Mountain Red Ware*, written in 1961 and published in 1970 (University of Arizona Press), has a heavy substantive content, and is still frequently cited. The nature of archaeology as an inexact science, and the need for re-synthesis by merging the old data with the new, could until recently only be accomplished through a printed written record.

Anthropological writing of the late nineteenth and twentieth centuries arose from different intellectual streams, natural history on the one hand and social philosophy on the other. Societies and cultures past and present were described and compared with goals of determining where they fit in history or how they worked. The historical school, founded by Franz Boas, frowned on premature speculation and emphasized the necessity of carefully collecting data on cultures and societies past and present before attempting synthesis. The goal, however, was synthesis and integration of the data about human beings derived from carefully collected data on human biology, prehistory, linguistics, society, and culture. The method of both preserving these data and communicating them to other researchers was mostly by writing supplemented by photographs and other illustrations, and publishing in journals and monographs. Writing is still required for communication today, but the internet offers a vastly expanded audience at little or no cost, whereas printing and distribution costs continue to accelerate. In 2017 the SFU library agreed to make electronic copies of all previously published *Archaeology Press* research monographs, and to put them online where they could be accessed by anyone for free. Are the types of printed journals and research monographs of the pre-electronic era still necessary, or has this method of data storage and communication become obsolete?

As the managing editor of *Archaeology Press* at Simon Fraser University for forty-five years (1972 to 2017) I oversaw the production, printing, and distribution of all our research monographs. The purpose was to make the information they contained available so it could be used by students and professionals. Many of these monographs were theses or derivatives of theses. The need to print theses disappeared when the university instituted the requirement that all theses be in electronic format so they could be put on line. Many other *Archaeology Press* monographs resulted from conferences or research projects. Today SFU Archaeology hosts few conferences and undertakes more archaeological research elsewhere than in the Pacific Northwest, and this change has also contributed to the demise of *Archaeology Press*.

Another factor in the decline of printed research in archaeology is the rise of the consulting industry in the last thirty years. Academic archaeology and consulting archaeology arise from different motivations.

Practitioners of the former are motivated by competition and cooperation with their peers and solving or adding to the puzzles of prehistory through wide distribution of their research. Consultants, on the other hand, need to make a monetary profit by satisfying the demands of a client, and wide distribution of their results is sometimes prohibited, usually unnecessary, and costly if published other than on the net. Academic publications do not usually require a profit, have sometimes been heavy on supply and low on demand, and still been available 50 or more years after they were initially printed. The Smithsonian was giving away free the remainder of its large surplus stock of BAE *Annual Reports* and *Bulletins* in the early 1950s (I ordered one of each), and many of the *Memoirs of the Jesup Expedition* were still available as least as late as 1956 (I ordered Tait's Thompson Indians).

The data of anthropology has become significantly different. When I was a student at the University of Washington (1950–1954) the Department of Anthropology was one of the four top anthropology departments in North America. The ethnography of non-literate native peoples was the primary database and was supplemented by physical anthropology, linguistics, and archaeology of these same peoples. By the time (1970) I instigated the split of archaeology from anthropology at Simon Fraser University, and formed the Department of Archaeology, there were very few non-literate native societies left anywhere in the world, and any salvage ethnography still being done was of questionable validity as an indicator of pre-contact culture. Socio-cultural anthropology had lost its data base, had shifted to the study of acculturation and current social problems, and had become less relevant to archaeology. Archaeology, on the other hand, had expanded during this period, largely triggered by incorporating many new techniques derived mostly from the hard sciences such as ^{14}C dating; there were still millions of archaeological sites throughout the world capable of supplying new data on the past. Cultural-historical and cultural-ecological synthesis has remained the ultimate research goal by anthropological archaeologists.

The primary purpose in writing and publishing research is still to make new data and ideas available to other scholars working on the same or similar problems. The internet now provides a more rapid and inexpensive technique for accomplishing this goal than does printing, and it is probable that institutions involved with the preservation and dissemination of archaeological and anthropological knowledge, as well as researchers themselves, will adapt even further to this technology. Writing, however, is still essential regardless of whether it is destined for the printed page or the air waves.

ESSAYS ON WRITING AND PUBLISHING

It's Writing, or Vacuuming

Alice B. Kehoe

Learn to Write Badly sums up the problem with academic writing. Students are still being taught to use the third person passive, to choose words barely anglicized from Greek and Latin, and, author Michael Billig's *bête noir*, to nominalize what doesn't in fact exist. Successful, sought-after academics disdain simple thoughts about actual data. For example, from current fads, "relational ontologies," "meshworks," "agency of substances and things," and "poiesis" describing "the Mississippianization of mid-continental... North Americans [which was] rhizomatic and afforded a more dramatic territorialization of relations once coordinated by people and cosmic forces at a higher scale. Whether some or all people intended at the beginning for this to happen seems both unlikely and beside the point" (Pauketat and Alt 2018:75). Did only "materialities" have agency, people did not?

Nowadays, with permanent academic positions continuing to be cut in favor of universities endlessly selling online courses monitored by TAs, fewer anthropologists need to publish. Fewer still have support from employers for time and research funding for fieldwork, followed by time to work up fieldnotes and data and construct publishable papers and books. Textbooks, more than ever, are products of a few large publishers whose staffs provide Technicolor photos, charts, online links, instructors' outlines and notes, and test questions. Anthropologists forced to teach four courses *a day* at two or three colleges each week, need such packages. They certainly have no time to write. Into the void come blogs, hastily done.

When I had my Ph.D., in 1964, I had published, in *American Antiquity*, a graduate independent research project analyzing sherds of the Northwestern Plains into wares and types. It was the first overview of ceramics in the region, my taxonomic labels have scientific priority, but only once were they cited, by a woman archaeologist; they were supplanted by rival systems created by ambitious Canadian men archaeologists. This has been the story for me, and for many women, the "invisible college" is a boys' school, women are literally not in their class, not heard nor seen (e.g., Bardolph 2014, Bardolph and Vanderwarker 2016). Women are less likely to write for publication when their published work, like themselves in person, are overlooked. This may change now that, since 2017, women are in the majority in Society for American Archaeology, and trending toward increasing numbers.

Why have I continued to write and seek to publish? I enjoy writing in scholarly style. I write easily, and those I consider true colleagues, actively engaged in research and thinking rather than career-building, compliment me on my writing. The bottom line, for me, is that when I am writing professionally, I feel I am taking a break from housework. Growing up, the expectation was clear that I would marry, have children, spend my life as a homemaker, little time for reading. "Nevertheless she persisted" in going to college and through graduate school. I obtained also the degree that seriously was openly advised for women wanting to do archaeology: the Mrs. That title offered opportunity to accompany the husband into the field, do the fieldwork chores, help with analyses, help with preparing reports, type them. Of course my husband did no household or childcare tasks. Nor could we afford hired help. Working intellectually instead of manually, hearing the typewriter ping instead of the vacuum's roar, was fulfilling, like eating chocolate.

It does help to feel impelled by wanting to say something. When I've worked from observational data through inference to what comes out as best explanation ("IBE"), I want to tell it to people. I'm skilled at that craft (I read history/philosophy/sociology of science, read history of our discipline, understand the principles of historical science). So I publish, though often not cited as I should be. A backward acknowledgment tends to happen when I comment at a lecture or presentation. The lords of the paradigm in vogue glare at me, make it clear that what I said was not welcome—once I was even physically pushed away (misdemeanor assault, it was). So I know that my assessment of the lords' work as fundamentally unscientific in terms of historical science, was correct: pushing dogma, they can't discuss what I offer.

This so far is my confession. It doesn't go into the difference between edited books of papers, and journal publication. For about twenty years now, most of my publications are essays or chapters in edited books. Colleagues invite me to contribute to volumes they're developing, on themes or topics or out of conference presentations; in a couple of cases, it's been an invitation to co-edit. An important distinction here is that submitting to journals is submitting to "peer" review by persons I might not consider my peers, whereas invitations to edited books are from like-minded colleagues. Established journals have high rates of rejection, because they get many more submissions than pages allotted to each volume of the journal. Journal editors tend to select papers that stay within the box, don't rock the boat. Edited book invitations spare me rejections because my paper doesn't fit mainstream expectations.

To sum up, I write easily and enjoy thinking as an anthropological archaeologist. Everything human is within our purview, there's no way to exhaust research possibilities nor interpretations. That's so much more rewarding than vacuuming the same damn rooms—now I can leave it to a student roomer, vacuuming in lieu of rent. For other anthropologists/archaeologists, the world is changing with online access. Anyone who enjoys writing can post. Ivory-tower denizens will go on with the latest obscurations (my online dictionary: "make unclear and difficult to understand"). It does bother me when the Theorists' juggernauts roll over people I know from the field, labeling them "animists" or "living always spiritually" or "foragers." With my books, I've tried to counter the imperialist impositions of such characterizations. I do wish more people read my efforts. When the end comes, I shall say that scoreboards on readers and citations didn't matter so much, writing was my pleasure stolen from my ordained life of housekeeping.

REFERENCES CITED

Bardolph, Dana N.
2014   A Critical Evaluation of Recent Gendered Publishing Trends in American Archaeology. *American Antiquity,* 79(3):522–540.

Bardolph, Dana N., and Amber M. Vanderwarker
2016   Sociopolitics in Southeastern Archaeology: The Role of Gender in Scholarly Authorship. *Southeastern Archaeology,* 53(3):175–193.

Billig, Michael
2013   *Learn to Write Badly: How to Succeed in the Social Sciences.* Cambridge, MA: Cambridge University Press.

Pauketat, Timothy R., and Susan M. Alt
2018   Water and Shells in Bodies and Pots: Mississippian Rhizome, Cahokian Poiesis. In *Relational Identities and Other-then-Human Agency in Archaeology*, edited by Eleanor Harrison-Buck and Julia A. Hendon, pp. 72–99. Louisville, CO: University Press of Colorado.

On Writing Paleozoology, Zooarchaeology, Archaeology, and in General

R. Lee Lyman

I published my first professional archaeology journal article in 1977. I was excited to be entering the ranks of professional archaeology, and publishing in one of the profession's peer-reviewed journals was, in my mind, symbolic of my credentials. I had completed my Master's thesis the year before and my first technical CRM report the year before that. I like to think I have become a much better writer since then, given the help of numerous astute reviewers of things I have submitted, including numerous technical reports, book chapters, book reviews, journal articles, and books. Another thing that helped along the way was the diversity of topics about which I have written. Different subjects and venues (and editors) require different structures to arguments and reasoning. I still get excited when my peers and journal editors think what I have written is worthy of publication, and I still get perturbed when they think otherwise (just ask my wife!), though not as much as I used to. There are things about writing and publishing that colleagues and students have prompted me to consider over the years that someone just entering the writing and publishing game should at least be aware of (forewarned about?) and, perhaps, think about. I outline a few of the more important of these things in the following.

First, readers of these comments are likely anthropologists, and as such, they are fully aware of the reality of individual differences. In the present context, my point is that some people write well from day one and others, such as myself, must work at it to become competent. Practice, and lots of it (along with feedback from others), is the only way to become adept at it. Academicians at many universities must write and publish because that is ~40% of their job; if they want to be promoted, win a raise in salary, or even hold their job into the future, they must publish in top-tier journals (these days measured with citation indices, impact factors, and rejection rates). That is a rule of the game made and enforced by university administrators. It is those administrators who seek prestige for their university because prestige allegedly encourages state legislators, donors, and funding agencies to pour more money into university coffers. But writing can also be gratifying to the author (see below). Of course I wrote because I wanted to be promoted and to earn raises. And I wrote for other reasons as well (see below).

Second, writing of any kind takes time, energy, thought (mental gymnastics), reading the pertinent literature, research, analysis, stringing words together, editing, and rewriting. It also requires development of a thick skin, to withstand criticisms of reviewers, many of whom force you to rethink and rewrite in a clear and efficient manner, others of whom you wonder if they actually read what you wrote. The most important point here is that reviewers will expose your weak thinking, incorrect analyses, mathematical mistakes, grammatical errors, every place you made a mistake from typographical errors through omission of a key reference to logical fallacies. This helps you become a better researcher as well as a better writer. Reviewers can be hurtful, whether or not that is their intention. This is so because writing for the public means you are exposing the intellectual and professional part of yourself, the part you hope your peers think is superb. As my doctoral advisor Donald Grayson said to me many years ago, "It is ok if your friends know you are an idiot, so ask them to unofficially review your manuscripts before submitting them to unknown members of your profession. You do not want the rest of the profession to know you are not very bright." Peer review is a good way to have your ego deflated, but it is also an exceptionally good way to learn both that you are not omnipotent and how to do research and write better.

Third, notice I said "learn you are not omnipotent." If you want to truly learn a subject, write something about it and submit it for peer review. If you are lucky, the peer reviewers will in no uncertain terms identify gaps in your knowledge, and the really good reviewers will also tell you how to fill the gaps they identify. Hence, you learn by writing. And that is another reason I write: I learn what I write about by reading as much as I can about the topic first. Then I have to write concisely and clearly about the topic; writing forces me to think clearly. Finally, reviewers tell me where I failed to learn sufficiently and think clearly. I learn some more by reading the literature I should have in the first place, doing the analyses I should have done in the first place, and writing about those things. Good writers are also good learners, and in any research field, it behooves us to never stop learning. Another benefit, one for my students rather than me, is that writing has helped me become a better teacher precisely because writing (and the research it requires) has forced me to learn topics inside-out, upside down, and frontwards and backwards. When a student asks a question, I either have a good answer at hand or I know how to find one *if* I have written a paper on that topic that withstood peer review. And this is yet another reason I write; it helped me be a better teacher.

Fourth, something you learn when trying to publish is persistence. I had a manuscript I thought was pretty good in the 1980s. I submitted it to an individual with knowledge of the topic and asked if he thought it was worthy of publication. He had a few comments and indicated that the manuscript was indeed worthy of publication. I submitted three versions of it to one journal; it was rejected every time, not always for good reason (in my view). I then sent the fourth edition to another journal that rejected it as inappropriate for that journal. So I then sent three other versions of it to a third journal that finally accepted for publication the seventh edition. It took nearly four years from the time of the first submission to acceptance. Not every experience I have had has been that lengthy; sometimes the second edition of a manuscript has been accepted. You will nevertheless learn persistence, just as I did. This does not mean, as Robson Bonnichsen once commented to me, that if a bit of research is worth doing and writing up, it is worth publishing. I do have several unpublished manuscripts that after a couple of unsuccessful submissions, have, since the last rejection, been sitting in my files for decades. Perhaps I could today write them in such a way as to make them acceptable to a journal editor somewhere, but my interests have shifted a bit from the topics of those papers and my current thinking about those topics is a bit murky and certainly out-of-date.

Finally, a couple students have over the past thirty-five years asked "How do you write (given it is time consuming and may require innovative thinking)?" A former graduate student by the name of Matthew Boulanger, whom I was working with at the time, laughed and gave an answer that I here share with you (with his permission). Boulanger provided the following series of steps (my elaborations are parenthetical) that describe the writing and publishing process:

How to Write and Publish:

1. Identify a research topic, phrase it as a question or testable hypothesis (this comes from discussions with your advisor or colleagues, or reading the pertinent literature).
2. Devise a way to evaluate or answer the question or test the hypothesis (this is the stage known as putting together a research design).
3. Do the research and analysis, and answer the question or test the hypothesis.
4. Write a paper discussing the question or hypothesis, describing your research design, and your analytical results. (It sometimes helps to know to which journal you are going to submit the manuscript for consideration as this may influence how you structure the paper.)
5. Format your paper for the journal you have chosen. (Each journal has a more or less unique format [e.g., the form of section headings, how references are cited, how reference lists are constructed].)
6. Submit to the chosen journal. (Virtually all journals now have online submission systems. You will need as well to have decided on 3–5 potential reviewers to recommend to the journal editor.)
7. Receive reviews of the manuscript (and either celebrate its acceptance and proceed to step 8, or have a stiff drink and begin figuring out how to appease the reviewers and make the editor happy). Revise and resubmit (hopefully only a time or two before celebrating).
8. Return to step 1.

Before I retired from academia, I taught a 1-credit course to first-year graduate students. One of the things we covered in that class was how to write research papers. There are many articles and books available that tell you how to do this. I examined a lot of these and chose several articles to have the students in my class read. These references are listed below. Take a look at them, then go to step 1 above and begin.

REFERENCES CITED

Boellstorff, Tom
2011   Submission and Acceptance: Where, Why, and How to Publish Your Article. *American Anthropologist*, 113:383–388.

Clapham, Phil
2005   Publish or Perish. *BioScience*, 55:390–391.

Donovan, Stephen K.
2005   The Joys of Peer Review or Do You Get the Willies When You Submit a Paper? *Palaios*, 20:99–100.

Gopen, George D., and Judith A. Swan
1990   The Science of Scientific Writing. *American Scientist*, 78:550–558.

Howitt, Susan M., and Anna N. Wilson
2014   Revisiting "Is the Scientific Paper a Fraud?" *Embo Reports*, 15:481–484.

Landes, Kenneth K.
1966   A Scrutiny of the Abstract, II. *Bulletin of the American Association of Petroleum Geologists*, 50:1992.

Medawar, P. B.
1964   Is the Scientific Paper a Fraud? *Listener*, 70:377–378. (Reprinted 1964, in *SR* [August]:42–43)

Sand-Jensen, Kaj
2007   How to Write Consistently Boring Scientific Literature. *Oikos*, 116:723–727.

Webster, R., and D. H. Yaalon
1994   The Research Paper: An Informal Guide for Authors. *Catena*, 21:3–11.

WHY DON'T WE WRITE MORE?

Writing to a More Inclusive Readership

Robert R. Mierendorf

As an anthropologist who uses mostly archaeological data to make inferences about past behavior, I've considered the questions about publishing anthropology from a perspective developed through career experiences, first as university-based consulting archaeologist, later as federal archaeologist and cultural resources manager, as teacher of field-based adult seminars on cultural history, as board member of an environmental education non-profit, and as private archaeological and cultural resource consultant, all in the Pacific Northwest. Many of these career activities overlap considerably with those of my professional colleagues. Practicing a form of public anthropology, I interacted closely with non-anthropologists and professionals in different disciplines, with tribal and first-nations representatives, with administrators and managers, and with the general public.

What Has Been Your Writing Philosophy?

Write with clarity and precision, and write anthropology not only to other professionals, but also for other public, nontechnical, educational, nonprofit, and governmental entities and audiences. Many such entities seek to learn from anthropological insights and how they might change perspectives, teaching curricula, and agency policies and planning. For writing to a more inclusive audience, I found mentors in disciplines outside of the one that molded my professional writing style. Individual writing styles usually adhere to professional standards and terminology, often defined more by particular disciplinary paradigms and less by any need to communicate to a larger, nonprofessional audience. Making the results of our efforts more comprehensible to other audiences fosters engagement of diverse communities in the work we do. The Society for American Archaeology and state offices promote professional outreach efforts, exemplified annually in the widespread practice of state-sponsored archaeology events geared to reach public audiences.

Archaeologists collect information and data to make inferences about places and natural spaces in a way few other disciplines do, but the challenge is to make insights available and understandable to audiences with no technical background. Many readers are discouraged by heavy data presentations, technical jargon, and abstractions that obscure the linkages between people in the past from those in the present, which in effect suppresses the local traditions and lived experiences of Indigenous communities.

What Has Motivated You to Write Professionally?

"So why would they do that?" The question was asked of me during one of many chance encounters with another backpacker, alone in an alpine meadow in the wilds of North Cascades National Park. The question came after I replied "archaeologist" in answer to his first inquiry. Squinting, he then asked, "Well what would you do?" These questions rank among the most frequent from park visitors over years of fieldwork in the park's backcountry. I learned that such inquiries reflected sincere attempts to understand why "they"—the National Park Service—would need anthropological or archaeological services in the middle of Wilderness.

Good questions from curious people made for stimulating impromptu discussion, but also made apparent to me the disconnect between popular perceptions of Wilderness and who might have been to such remote places before them, or not. The common appellation spawned in "sublime" alpine scenery that "I was surely the first to cast eyes on…" represents another common denial of the landscape's prior human history. Hence the notion of an Indigenous history would often arouse expressions of surprise or sometimes momentary meditations on what such a history might mean. It made no sense to me that this notion should surprise, yet it highlighted again the need of interpreting the cultural past for general audiences.

I also gained from other more enduring discussions, many of them lighted by camp fires in the Upper Skagit or Stehekin River valleys, in field seminars attended by an array of participants seeking knowledge about mountain history. These campfire and classroom exchanges and knowledge sharing moments revealed to me high levels of interest and appreciation, conveyed in particular by elementary and high school teachers, who found it difficult to first access, and then make classroom use of current knowledge about pre-contact histories and Indigenous ethnographies in their own teaching districts, localities, valleys, and watersheds.

These encounters motivated me to reach audiences, from outside of the profession, who sought a deeper understanding of the archaeology and ethnography of Pacific Northwest places. My employer at the time, the National Park Service, further encouraged outreach activities aligned with its mission of public "interpretation" (education) of national parks. My interactions frequently entailed the simple breaking down of stereotypes of archaeologists (mostly perpetuated by media, some by archaeologists), of what they do, and of what they look for—conservation archaeology, site protection and stabilization, and traditional cultural values and landscapes are foreign concepts at first-hearing. Sometimes the questions came from my government co-workers with expertise in other fields and sometimes from members and affiliates of Tribes and First Nations. Others included high school teachers, college faculty, and book writers. The need for answers sought by these audiences seemed to match closely the educational and "outreach" imperatives of several disciplines, including archaeology: to encapsulate the results of research in a form comprehensible to a general audience. Increasingly specialized studies producing new data coupled with its rapid dissemination only deepens the need for synthesis and for the technical to be made less so, if goals for expanded audience insight, appreciation, participation, and support are to be attained.

What Challenges Have You Had to Overcome to Get Published?

Challenges include finding the "right" publisher, i.e., one that meets author needs for audience, data presentation format, open access versus other options, color printing, and cost. Too often, publisher style guidelines and international journal formats dictate how data are displayed in ways incompatible with the scope of a study. Other options, such as a monograph (e.g., *Journal of Northwest Anthropology's Memoir Series*) or occasional series, may offer lower cost and higher readership access compared to international journals. More than ever, electronic access factors into selection of a publisher.

What Suggestions Do You Have for Would-be Writers?

As in any writing, be certain of your target audience, of what to convey to them, and of the means for doing so. Beyond proficiency in publishing technical reports and peer-reviewed articles, there are opportunities to write to a less technical and broader readership. If that is an interest, be open to other publishing formats, or to those with a general audience or theme, such as John Miles' edited book of "Naturalist" essays of reflections on varied environmental and cultural perspectives of North Cascades landscapes (Mierendorf 1996; Miles 1996). Some publishers seek writers who make comprehensible and give contextual meaning to current issues that anthropologists and archaeologists are equipped to address. In one example, editors of an archaeology encyclopedia published concise essays about archaeological places in America, including in Washington State (McManamon 2009: V. 3 and 4), in order to fill a gap in student and public education about archaeology. In another, the Gilder Lehrman Institute of American History's online journal for teachers published a theme issue on archaeology's role in reconstructing the American past (History Now 2017). Sometimes agencies commemorate events or anniversaries of special places, and in the case of Manning Provincial Park's 50th anniversary, seek to acknowledge the long Indigenous history and ties to the lands being commemorated (Mierendorf 1991). Though of small format, such low circulation special publications reach a select audience and reassert Tribal and First Nation's narratives of traditional places in today's mountain preserves.

Experience suggests that a career in archaeology and anthropology means it's likely you will be asked to write nontechnical narratives of several sorts or genres—such requests can present opportunities. Like a second language, a writing proficiency exercised in a less technical genre than that of one's profession enlarges the circle of sharing and compels increased appreciation for anthropology's contributions. To start, it's easy to enroll in writing workshops and to talk with writers about writing, including creative and informed nonfiction, "interpretive" materials, "popular" brochures, commemorative publications, and assorted journalistic genres. In addition to colleagues in archaeology and anthropology, I've consulted cultural and natural history writers including Ruth Kirk, Robert Michael Pyle, and William Dietrich. Gary Snyder, environmentalist, poet, and anthropologist, encouraged and advised to "write much" during our tour of the Upper Skagit River valley in 2002.

How Can We as a Profession Ensure That Anthropologists in the Pacific Northwest of All Types and Backgrounds Continue to Publish?

Lend support to publishers of journals, monograph and memoir series, books, and occasional publications that anthropologists and others in related fields use to disseminate results of investigations. A stable membership base that readily submits articles for publication is necessary to ensure viable publication outlets. Such support may be even more critical for publishers of smaller regional journals compared with those supported by large national and international memberships.

REFERENCES CITED

History Now
2017   Gilder Lehrman Institute of American History, https://www.gilderlehrman.org/history-now/2017-11/excavating-american-history.

McManamon, Francis P. (General Editor)
2009   *Archaeology in America An Encyclopedia.* Vols. 1–4, Greenwood Press, Westport, CT.

Mierendorf, Robert R.
1991   An Archeologist's View. In *Manning Park Memories, Reflections of the Past*, pp. 15–19, Ministry of Lands and Parks, Province of British Columbia.

1996   Who Walks on the Ground. In *Impressions of the North Cascades*, John C. Miles (Ed), pp. 39–53, The Mountaineers, Seattle.

Miles, John C. (Editor)
1996   *Impressions of the North Cascades.* The Mountaineers, Seattle.

A Writing Philosophy

Mark G. Plew

I think my writing philosophy has much to do with the importance that people around me placed upon it. In my case, I had the good fortune to study with and be around people for whom reporting and publishing were paramount—even more importantly believed as my mentor did that publishing on one's work should be undertaken promptly. I was, I believe, fortunate to have been encouraged even as an undergraduate to write and to think about publishing. Having been encouraged to read exhaustively has helped improve my writing many fold. Though we are professionally motivated to publish for a number of reasons, not the least of which is promotion and tenure, I have found that consistent writing has made me a better thinker. I have seen writing as an important part of my professional and personal development and something that I have always thought should always be contributing. For that reason, I have very rarely undertaken projects that I didn't think would lead to better or more complete understandings of a problem. For that reason, I have rarely presented papers that I did not intend to see through to publication.

There are today a number of issues relating to anthropological publishing that pertain to individuals but also journals. As a state journal editor, I have seen a marked reduction in the number of submissions over the past decade. Although we might attribute this in part to more grey literature reporting or an increasing number of publishing outlets, there are notably fewer contributions from graduate students and academic faculty, and even fewer from those working in cultural resource management. Although there are notable exceptions, there are too few within the community who publish—something problematic given the quantities of data generated by their efforts. I find that there is and has been a growing sense of this not being a requirement of their professional lives; academics probably deserve some responsibility for this. To ensure that regional anthropologists continue to publish requires those of us in academic positions to encourage our students to begin thinking about publishing early in their careers. This may require us to invest more time in helping students conduct research projects that lead not to posters and conference presentations alone, but to publications. My personal experience is that those who get an early start don't fear the review process that drives many from submitting their work. I also think that editors need to be more proactive in encouraging submissions—especially from cultural resource managers. Finally, I wonder if the trend toward multiple authored papers is not a factor in the reduction of submissions.

ESSAYS ON WRITING AND PUBLISHING

Part 2

Part 2 contains the following essays:

- "Eschew BS and Insist on Disclosure" by Thomas F. King, Ph.D. in anthropology from the University of California, who has worked for the last 50+ years in archaeology and historic preservation, in government and in the private sector, in the United States and the Pacific Islands; a reformed former U.S. government employee, now self-employed as a cultural heritage and environmental impact assessment consultant based in Silver Spring, Maryland. King has written twelve textbooks and tradebooks, nine monographs, two novels, and sixty journal articles.
- "To Publish or Not to Publish—The Changing Nature of Archaeology" by Dennis Griffin, the State Archaeologist with the Oregon State Historic Preservation Office where he has worked since 2002. He received his Ph.D. in Anthropology from the University of Oregon in 1999 and has spent over 40 years working throughout the Pacific Northwest. His areas of interest focus in the Pacific Northwest and Alaska with a specialization in oral history, tribal collaborative research, and more recently, Oregon's early military history. Griffin has published two books, twenty articles in refereed journals, one book review, thirteen articles in non-refereed publications, two book chapters, and well over one hundred-forty technical reports.
- "If You Dig a Site, You Must Record in Detail *and* Write Up Results, Since Your Site Area is Now Gone Forever...." by Dale R. Croes, B.A. in anthropology from the University of Washington (UW), M.A. and Ph.D. in anthropology at Washington State University. He did his Ph.D. dissertation research on basketry and cordage artifacts from the Ozette Village wet site. Adjunct Professor, Anthropology, Washington State University, Director, Pacific Northwest Archaeological Society and Services . Croes has authored eight books and fifty-eight articles.
- "*Caveat Emptor*, Anthropology is a Lifetime of Writing" by Kevin J. Lyons, thirty-year practitioner of ethno-archaeology in Interior Pacific Northwest anthropology. Serving as the Kalispel Tribe of Indians' Cultural Resources Program Manager for the past twenty years; good days are filled with primary ethnographic research,

medium days are filled with archaeological analysis, and tedious/necessary days are filled with administrative and/or policy work. He has contributed to Pei-Lin Yu's 2015 anthology "Rivers, Fish, and the People" provided editing assistance to John Ross' 2011 ethnography "The Spokan Indians," and has penned the usual administrative detritus that is cultural resources management copy.

- "Some Hidden Facets of Writing Archaeology" by Madonna L. Moss, Professor of Anthropology at the University of Oregon and Curator of Zooarchaeology at the UO Museum of Natural and Cultural History. She received her Ph.D. in 1989 from University of California, Santa Barbara. Moss has authored or co-authored over 80 peer-reviewed articles, written two books and two monographs, and has published dozens of non-peer-reviewed articles.
- "Writing Tensions: Voices That Help—and Those That Don't" by Mark S. Warner, Professor of anthropology at the University of Idaho and the president of the Society for Historical Archaeology (2018–2019). He is a historical archaeologist and his research interests include issues of inequality, the American West, zooarchaeology and foodways and collections management. He is the author of *Eating in the Side Room: Food, Archaeology and African American Identity* (2015), and co-editor (with Margaret Purser) of *Historical Archaeology through a Western Lens* (2017). Warner has authored or coedited four books and two thematic issues of journals, as well as authored or coauthored nineteen articles and book chapters.
- "From Writing Science to Writing for the General Public" by Dennis Dauble, retired fisheries scientist and adjunct professor at Washington State University Tri-Cities. He earned a B.S. and doctorate in fisheries from Oregon State University and a M.S. in biology from Washington State University. Dauble has authored sixty journal articles, forty-eight technical reports, the natural history guidebook *Fishes of the Columbia River Basin*, and three short-story collections.

ESSAYS ON WRITING AND PUBLISHING

Eschew BS and Insist on Disclosure

Thomas F. King

Writing—particularly writing fiction—vies with field archaeology as the most fun I've had with my pants on. I write because I like to, and I've been blessed to be able to make a living doing it.

I don't know that my writing's guided by any explicit philosophy, but I'm happiest with work that I think is elegant, that's clever, that communicates with people in plain language about something that's important at some level. If I have a writing philosophy, I guess it would be to eschew BS.

Getting published has often been a challenge for me—usually for good reason. Now that I'm no longer trying to build a resumé, I pretty much write for publication only if asked, and otherwise satisfy myself with my weblogs, occasional Huffington Post pieces, and postings to Academia.edu.

My impression is that in today's world of anthropological publishing, there are lots of places to publish but a good many discouragements to doing so. One of these is what seems to me to be the widespread demand for adherence to postmodern styles, which combine a snooty insistence on inclusive discourse with terminology that enforces exclusivity. Another is the discomfort that some communities feel for being written about, and for having their ancestors' lifeways plumbed. Another is that much anthropological—especially archaeological—writing is done under contract for commercial entities and others who reflexively seek to impose non-disclosure requirements, to which government and the professional community have offered only the most flaccid pushback.

My advice to would-be anthropological writers, I suppose, would be "just do it." Write about what interests you. Try to have fun with your writing, whether it's a journal, field notes, an email to a friend, a social media posting, a contract report, an essay, or a novel. Keep a journal, and in it try to practice "thick description" (c.f. https://en.wikipedia.org/wiki/Thick_description). And read some good anthropological writing; off the top of my head I'd suggest Keith Basso's "Wisdom Sits in Places" (1996) and Margery Wolf's "Coyote's Country" (2018), but there are plenty of other examples. Keep throwing your writing at others, for publication or just to share. Throw nothing away that you've written; you can digitize and discard hard copies, but don't let your words be destroyed. They'll be useful to someone, someday, as a record of the times if nothing else.

As to what the Pacific Northwest anthropological profession can do to encourage publication, I'm of at least a couple of minds. I think it's worth discussing what does and does not NEED to be published in a traditional sense. How many dead-tree journals do we need any more? What alternatives to publication should the academic and related communities accept to forestall perishment?

As I've watched my own dead-tree publications fall into disuse and obscurity, and seen the price of acquiring or accessing them ascend into the ionosphere, I've become more and more convinced that academia's fixation with traditional publication is misguided and counterproductive. Publication has traditionally served two purposes in and around academia. It has preserved and communicated data and ideas, and it has been a context for discussion and debate. There are now many alternatives to the dead-tree book or journal as means of serving both functions. Some are more cost-effective than others, but I'm guessing that dead-tree publication is about as cost-ineffective as options come. *JONA* has not only a distinguished journal but a fine worldwide website with lots of links; maybe there are ways to make that site more accessible, more widely used by the community, and use it to encourage writing of all types.

Then there's the matter of those non-disclosure provisions in CRM contracts. There's seldom much reason for their inclusion; it's just something that private firms tend to do. The anthropological community, I think, should take a firm stand against the use of such instruments except where their use serves a pretty clear public interest. Sometimes they do serve such interests, but often they do not. It's obviously a discouragement to publication when one writes something that one thinks is useful and worthy, and then cannot share it with others who might find it so. I imagine that CRM practitioners in the Northwest would benefit from *JONA*'s taking a seriously skeptical attitude toward prohibitions on public disclosure.

To Publish or Not to Publish—The Changing Nature of Archaeology

Dennis Griffin

There are many reasons one can hypothesize why writing has fallen off among archaeologists, young and old. Such a change could be due to changes that have occurred in academia and the mentoring relationship that historically developed between students and teachers, or the evolving world of cultural resource management (CRM) where most students find themselves working after graduation. Since the time that I was a young college student, universities have changed their expectations of teachers requiring them to place an emphasis on publishing over teaching in order to earn tenure, with such publications often being solo authored and directed toward national over regional publications to attract a wider audience. This change occurred at the same time as an increase in general class size, a switch to computer graded exams over the earlier required essays and class papers, a rise in on-line degrees, a reduction in research opportunities for students to work with faculty that equates to reduced opportunities for students to develop close mentoring relationships with teachers, and less of a focus on writing within the classroom environment. All of these changes, in addition to the effects of less focus on grammar and writing skills during primary and secondary education add up to students who often do not see publishing as an integral part of their career unless they choose to be a teacher in a university setting. Fewer graduate students appear to recognize the importance of publishing an article on their thesis research; something they have spent two to three or more years of their lives slaving over and only want to put it behind them and get on to gainful employment.

In the world of CRM since the mid-1980s, project related archaeological contracts have largely passed from the universities to private CRM firms with work becoming highly competitive and now tied to stricter budgets and tighter time frames for completion. Report writing has also changed where it has now become rare for project reports to be written by a single author with writing being divvied up among multiple writers, not in a collaborative way that had been the norm within a university setting, but where different authors are assigned their own chapter of a report with little opportunity to deal with a project in its entirety. Analyzes have become more compartmentalized with no single person being able to summarize the totality of research. Due to the competitive cycle of CRM projects, staff are forced to move directly on to other pressing projects with little time to write articles for journals that aren't required by a contract. As a result, fewer authors choose to publish the results of their research.

I was fortunate to have been taught early in my professional archaeological career that if a job is worth doing it is worth telling others about. This sentiment often came from professors that did not themselves publish much aside from grey-literature reports but they chose to use their classroom as a forum to disseminate the results of their own research as well as that of others that impressed them about the topic of the daily classroom discussions. These teachers strongly encouraged students to present at local regional conferences with their university providing free transportation to such conferences, cheap shared lodging (often filling the floor with students in sleeping bags), employed students as research assistants, and encouraged them to author or coauthor papers on the projects they assisted with. University anthropology clubs often had forums available where we were able to share our research with fellow students, while working to perfect our analyses and results and sharpen our delivery. Having a general fear of speaking in front of large audiences, I forced myself to try and present at least one paper at a conference each year in order to combat such fears, and if the responses were good to try and later publish it. I find that there is no better way to force oneself to pool one's thoughts on a topic into a cohesive document then facing a conference schedule or classroom assignment. We were given many opportunities to write in graduate school, as it was not unusual to have three 20-page papers due each term. My writing may not have been very good but I certainly learned to write *a lot*.

After working at a State Historic Preservation Office (SHPO) for over sixteen years, I have had the rare opportunity to review and read through hundreds of reports each year summarizing archaeological projects within Oregon. Many of these are associated with small CRM projects that lack a larger regional perspective and would not normally be suitable for publication in journals or monographs. However, each year a number of larger projects produce multi-volume reports with many different research variants that would be excellent for publication. Unfortunately, few ever see the light of day aside from grey literature reports that are shared with the company that hired the authors, and if shared with SHPO, are scanned and available only on the state's on-line archaeological inventory to qualified archaeologists. I feel this is largely due to the pressure authors have to be able to move quickly on to new projects and a general lack of desire in scholarship where funding is not available to pay for the time it would take to write up and share the results of projects.

What suggestions would I have for would-be writers? First, I would remind students that if they thought their master's thesis research was important enough to spend several years completing, that they aren't the only one that would think so. Each year I hear many excellent thesis or project-related presentations at NWAC and other regional conferences and I strongly encourage authors to attempt to share their findings. Many of us would love to learn more about their research and if we missed their conference presentation or were unable to decipher the richness of their research from their conference title or abstract we may never hear of it. Finding a journal to publish your writing is not the problem; it is getting your thoughts down on paper and seeking to share your research in the first place. Many state archaeology associations have journals that are begging for articles.

Second, remember why it is that you chose archaeology as your profession. It certainly wasn't for the money or the ability to spend your days working in an 8am to 5pm office environment. You probably read something that caught your interest and got you thinking this is what I want to do! For me, archaeology provided me with a means to travel the world working with and studying people of different cultures. Seeing the changes that occurred to cultures over time, whether they be large-scale changes resulting from outside culture contact and disease, changes in resource availability or the effects of climate change, or the simple evolution of a particular style of can or bottle label was both exciting and stimulating. Having an insatiable curiosity, I find topics that draw my interest almost on a daily basis and the problem is not what topic to research and write about but which other topics do I have to put aside in order to focus on getting the first written.

Third, consider working with a tribe or different cultural group in order to gain a different perspective from your own. I think writing stems from the realization that your perceptions, ideas and insights are different than what you read every day.

What can we as a community do to encourage publishing? One thing might be to offer to publish a proceeding from each year's Northwest Anthropology Conference, much like is done at the Chacmool Archaeological Conference in Calgary, Alberta. I don't think the publication of such a proceeding would seriously affect submissions to existing regional journals such as *JONA*, while it would provide an opportunity for students and non-student archaeologists to see their research in print. The proceeding would not need to be peer-reviewed, thus reducing an author's fear of their research being seriously criticized. After seeing their work in print, authors would be encouraged to submit their work to peer-reviewed journals as the next logical step. I know that NWAC moves around each year and places many demands on the school or agency that sponsors each year's conference, but the publication of a conference proceeding could be offered to the local Anthropology Club as an opportunity to gain hands-on experience in editing and publishing while gaining them recognition for their editing efforts.

A second idea would be to require the publication of the results of all archaeology mitigation projects. If a significant site is being adversely affected by a project and mitigation is required, aside from data recovery or other mitigation measures, make the publication of an article in a regional or national journal or local newspaper a stipulation of the MOA.

If the public does not understand and support cultural resource protection, future administrations may make legislative changes that limit its continued protection. Sharing the results of mitigation projects will serve to educate the public about local history, increase support for archaeology, and encourage authors to publish future articles about their research even when not required.

If You Dig a Site, You Must Record in Detail *and* Write Up Results, Since Your Site Area is Now Gone Forever

Dale R. Croes

Trained as an archaeological scientist, it was instilled early (I think by Dr. Robert Ackerman, Washington State University (WSU) who has an exemplary record of reporting his work) that one "should not dig, unless you write-up your findings." The excavation part, and for me hydraulic wet site excavations, were always an adventure—you never knew what wood and fiber artifacts you might find—though painstaking in terms of the scientific recording. The meticulous recording was also primary, since we certainly destroy the part of the site we excavate as a "non-renewable resource." Therefore, writing started with the documentation so one could synthesize all the notes into a summary report. I guess if you follow all the rules of the scientific approach, especially recording one's observations and detailing how one develops and classifies systematically what you find, writing starts there. Then you try to present the hard part, explaining what you found, then you need to try to outline eloquently your hypotheses.

I don't consider myself a natural writer, put do enjoy the process. I had some good English teachers as a University of Washington undergraduate and was introduced to the "little" book by William Strunk, Jr., and E. B. White, *The Elements of Style* (1959). Fortunately it was "little" and I still have that tattered copy I used to carry around in my back pocket while in Basic and Advanced Infantry training in the Army. When we had breaks, I often pulled it out and learned a new lesson. I had joined the reserves and so I returned to graduate school to work on writing my WSU M.A. thesis and Ph.D. dissertation after the 4.5 months of training. So, I had to work at becoming a writer and still must go through several drafts when writing, though I enjoy editing and back-and-forth with reviewers/editors too.

What Has Motivated You to Write Professionally?

Again, my professional motivation has been to be sure and write-up the archaeological sites I have been responsible for directing and all the endless pieces of data recovered from the site, therefore fulfilling my archaeological and scientific professional responsibility. I proudly say that I have finished, with lots of help from teams of researchers, all four of the sites I have directed in my career, so can retire without guilt or the ongoing responsibility of getting it written up. Now it is writing what I want to compile, which has been a synthesis of my and Ed Carriere's, a Suquamish Elder and Master Basketmaker, life histories, testing my career hypotheses, and re-assessing old basketry collections like Biderbost (see next part).

Benefits of Writing Memoir 15—Re-Awakening Ancient Salish Sea Basketry, Fifty Years of Basketry Studies in Culture and Science (2018) with Ed Carriere, Suquamish Elder and Master Basketmaker.

[I ended the last submission saying that if we don't publish our archaeological field work, we should not have even excavated, since now it is gone forever; I kept this to the allotted 1,000 words. Then I was asked to write about the trials, tribulations, and hopefully benefits of writing a *JONA* memoir (*Memoir* 15) in partnership (50/50) with Ed Carriere, where we described our lifetime work on basketry in culture and science:]

What started out to be a post-retirement scientific re-assessment of 2,000-year-old Biderbost wet site (45SN100) basketry at the UW Burke Museum, (a collection I recorded in a rush in a Washington Archaeological Society (WAS) garage "lab" in 1973 for my Ph.D. dissertation), took a totally unimagined turn. Normally I would re-examine each ancient basketry piece (after 45 years of growing experience and new assistance of Kathleen Hawes conducting cellular ID on each piece (not possibly before)) and write it up as a technical report. Then a flash of enlightenment crossed my mind; I needed to call my friend Ed Carriere, Suquamish Elder and Master Basketmaker, and suggest he join us and try to replicate what represented his 100th grandparent's baskets from Biderbost. The thought certainly caught his imagination and triggered the writing of a book (*JONA Memoir* 15) on his and my 50 years of focus on basketry, me as an archaeological scientist and him as a cultural career expert.

After Kathleen, Ed and I met at the Burke, having secured permission from Laura Phillips, the Archaeological Collections Manager, the magic happened; Ed analyzed each piece of basketry from Biderbost, synthesizing in his mind how to replicate the most complex pack basket that Laura challenged him to re-construct, and Kathleen let him know that the basketry material used at the site to make these baskets was almost exclusively split cedar root. That is all he needed to know, and he went to work while on vacation at a time-share he has in Mexico, packing his bag full of split and processed cedar roots.

Upon return we talked by phone and he was excited to show me the large, replicated, fine-gauge, open-twined pack basket he carefully made; I quickly got into my car and drove the hour and a half north to his home studio and was truly impressed and knew we were onto something anthropologically big. He loved learning from his ancestors, which was usually up to five to six generations back, and now he did something he had never dreamed of: work with a master weaver, and no doubt grand relative, one-hundred generations back. My statistical analyses of all ancient Northwest Coast basketry clearly showed the linkage of style in Ed's traditional Salish Sea territory up to one-hundred fifty generations back, verifying scientifically the strong cultural transmission of basketry traditions through Ed's teacher, who raised him from infancy, his Great Grandmother Julia Jacobs, to him. The book was a matter of synergizing this combined culture and science work through our life stories.

Ed and I thought this to be a good idea to compile a book, and he was very patient in our transcribing, in his voice, over half of the manuscript presentation. Since the Ozette project (my M.A. and Ph.D. work), I had learned to work in equal partnership with Tribes in my ongoing professional career, and knew this book with Ed had to be an equal partnership, which it is. This included my replicating the basic, checker-work, ancient pack baskets from Biderbost, with Ed's guidance and from what I had learned in Makah basketry classes as part of my Ozette research.

I also had to "excavate" through vast amounts of Ed's and my images/photos to capture this history, which somehow worked. Fortunately I had visited Ed as often as possible over the past twenty-four years while teaching at South Puget Sound Community College and began recording a lot of his early works in photographic detail. Ed was an amateur photographer through his life, which really helped in compiling his amazing history. Fortunately I was retired in 2013 from the time consuming and hard task of teaching, and have been blessed with the time over the past five years to work essentially full time with Ed on this project.

Writing is one thing, publishing is another. So much of this involves being lucky, and persistent. We compiled a manuscript fully illustrated with photographs and line-drawings and began showing potential publishers. The Northwest Tribes had taken a great interest in this project, especially the Northwest Native American Basketweavers Association (NNABA) and had us present our progress on replicating the ancient Salish Sea baskets at each of their main annual meetings. Their NNABA Board passed a resolution to write a letter supporting the detailed publication of our work. We had meetings with both Western and Eastern Washington publishers associated with Universities and the first said "there is no audience for this book" and the second said that we would have to strip most of the illustrations and take out anything that was not basketry (such as Ed's detailed canoe carving). I pondered the "no audience" statement and told Ed the Tribes wanted this published and could care less about who the audience is, and the greatly reduced (illustration-wise) idea would loss a lot of the detail the Tribes wanted too.

As mentioned, publishing takes a lot of luck and persistence, and I thought of checking with an old friend, Dr. Darby Stapp, owner of Northwest Anthropology LLC, and the publication started to materialize. He embraced the idea and the over 300 color images seemed no problem to him. He took our five-chapter manuscript and worked it over into ten chapters with our time-line of Ed's and my lifetime study of basketry. The book finally came together better than Ed or I had imagined. Darby Stapp and Julie Longenecker have an amazing and talented staff of designers and editors, bringing together a book NNABA and Tribes liked very much.

And we realized we were taking a new approach in Northwest Anthropology/Archaeology that could be applied elsewhere; we demonstrated how this equal partnership, both cultural experts and archaeological sciences, could show how these ancient basketry artifacts create ideational links via shared ideas through hundreds of Salish Sea generations. Truly what archaeology strives to do is show how their database, artifacts, reflect how ideas are shared through long-term cultural transmission; how humans actually operated through the generations as demonstrated by the artifacts we find. This is more than *experimental archaeology* or *ethnoarchaeology* and we decided to call it *Generationally-Linked Archaeology* (GLA).

Knowing the Tribal interest was our main book audience, I submitted 1% casino grants to the Squaxin Island Tribe and they provided us funds to send book to all Northwest libraries and colleges. I also submitted to other tribes to subsidize the book so Tribal members could get the book at about half price. The Siletz, Tulalip and Snoqualmie gave Northwest Anthropology LLC, this support.

Following the book release Ed and I have enjoyed sharing the work with both scientific and Indigenous audiences, taking all our replicated baskets and samples with us, finding good reception from both. Our first coming out and book signing was with the Musqueam Band in Vancouver, B.C., Canada followed by the UBC Museum of Anthropology (MOA) opening the next night. Since Musqueam and UBC MOA 3,000–4,500-year-old wet site basketry really crystallized our idea for the GLA approach, and since the UW Burke Museum was busy moving to their new museum, we were glad to open in B.C. Following this opening we went to the Northwest Anthropology Conference (NWAC), The Society for American Archaeology (SAA), and a Wetland Archaeology Conference in central France—all professional groups. With an invitation from the Maori National Weavers Gathering we went to New Zealand with Ed's apprentice Josh Mason, Squaxin Island Tribe, to present our work. One of our favorite presentations is with the Northwest Native American Basketweavers Association, and we consider this a NNABA book because of their ongoing support. We also recognize that the Biderbost site is in Snoqualmie Tribe traditional territory and presented our book and work to their Elder's Honoring, where they purchased 100 of our books and gave them out for signing to their members; they are truly excited to get back their 100th grandparent's and Master Basketmaker's work.

We also recently traveled to Juneau Alaska through Sealaska corporation to present our work and to be in classes with their Master Haida basketmaker, Delores Churchill. The American Museum of Natural History asked us to come to New York and help them with the re-model of their Northwest Coast Hall, originally developed by Dr. Frans Boas (father of American Anthropology), for its 150th Anniversary of this Hall.

Ed's Suquamish Museum is opening a show on our work starting in mid-January 2019 through mid-June 2019. His community is very proud of his accomplishments through the years and excited about the new book documenting his amazing cultural contributions. They got loans of the ancient wet site baskets from UBC MOA, UW Burke, and Squaxin Museums—try to attend!

Upcoming professional programs will be the NWAC, SAA and the 11th Experimental Archaeology Conference (EAC11) in Trento, Italy, where Ed and I have been asked to keynote the event. All this currently upcoming events will feature discussions of our approach, *Generationally-Linked Archaeology*.

Therefore writing this book has provided Ed and I many opportunities to travel and visit with Indigenous artisans and professional archaeologists throughout the world. When we think back in the process to the publisher that said "there is no audience for this book," we are happy to report there has been both Indigenous and professional interest in our writing this *Generationally-Linked Archaeology* book in equal partnership.

A good review of the book is from BC Booklook: https://bcbooklook.com/2019/01/08/462-baskets-across-the-border/ and a Hakai Online Magazine article is available at: https://hakaimagazine.com/features/the-basketmaker/

Some past publications with some links from author's WSU Anthropology web page: *https://anthro.wsu.edu/documents/2017/09/dale-croes-2.pdf*

Caveat Emptor, Anthropology is a Lifetime of Writing

Kevin J. Lyons

Anthropology is not an essential. Bet no one in graduate school mentioned that to you. It, and the many social activities that we lavish our time with, does not defend the frontier, protect the innocent from injustice, feed the hungry, or mend the ill. Nonetheless, there is a social good that is provided by its various practitioners through the exposition of how humanity is a unifiable whole with both a common ancestry and destiny. That social good can only be delivered when the time spent results in a publicly accessible product that makes the efforts of our peers more efficient and demonstrates the virtues that anthropology can uniquely communicate to our sponsors the public. With those admissions voiced, why then is the state of anthropological publication in such a shabby state? It is not for a lack of venues; how many top tier journals are publishing content well outside their titled domains? It is not a technological issue; portions of this essay I scribbled on post-it notes at a laundromat, on a memo application on my cell phone while riding a bus, forwarding such content to my cloud account and complied on to a free online word-processing platform. When the means of production are both free and ubiquitous, coupled with content starved channels, I infer the lack of production to be the fault of the anthropologists. When I see such behavioral signatures among the novice, I assume one of two fundamental causations: fear of ridicule, or an inability to connect the strategic vision of anthropology with the necessary and mundane acts that deliver anthropology to the sponsoring public. I am less forgiving of myself and other seasoned anthropologists when we fail to write. At the end of days, being an anthropologist is committing to a life of research, reading, writing, editing, and coaching the successor generations of anthropologist. This is the trade craft of anthropology and pursuing the strategic vision that humanity is worthy of understanding in all its variety circumstances.

As per the instructions of our beneficent editor, I'm to keep this essay short, useful, and blunting my vicious pen; each instruction contrary to my norm. If you are new to the trade and overly concerned that you'll not hit a home run at your first at bat and that's what is holding you back, then I hope this serves. All writers' first drafts are crap, it's editing that shapes the rough and not ready for others into something that has the potential to shine a light on the good that anthropology provides. Many novices are aware of this and make a fundamental error of editing while drafting copy. This cannot be done with any efficiency, consistency, and/or economy. Editing is a repetitive act that follows the act of writing. Writing is fundamentally a creative and deeply emotional act; your voice will leak out of your pen, which always tempts a writer to defend each verb and noun with too much zeal. Editing is the coldhearted act of "killing darlings," adhering to publication ethics and standards, assuring the writer's ego does not abuse the readers' attention, and demands narrative economy and clarity. In short, they are very different uses of your brain and contrary to any self-delusion you and others suffer, humans don't multi-task well. I could cite all the neuroscience research that supports this opinion but *tempus fugit*.

As to making that home run on your first at bat, it's not going to happen. Epic performance is the result of epic preparation; the anthropological "industry" does not expect a novice to be a master of the trade on their first day. Mastery, the effortless command of hundreds of micro-skills, only develops after years of continual use of those micro-skills. When I look at the copy I wrote some three decades ago, I cringe at the clumsy, inconsiderate, and inefficient narration of simple questions and the methods used to explore them. Accept that in your early days as an anthropologist, you are traveling a long road that consists of researching, reading, writing, and editing. Call these the essential macro-skills of being an anthropologist. Nested within the writing macro-skill there are the following micro-skills: organization, consistency, staying on topic, closing loops, and following through.

As to the micro-skill of consistency, for comparative purposes, modern American novelists have an average daily production of 1,000 word count a day with the average novel consisting of 100,000 words. The more prolific modern novelists (e.g., Stephen King) self-report an average of 6,000 words a day. My best performance was 8,000 words a day for 14 consecutive days, a feat I shall not repeat as it was mentally exhausting and in retrospect the product was self-indulgent dribble. There are two points to underline here; consistent measured effort nets actionable results and the motivated writer can achieve considerable volume of rough copy in reasonable time. If just starting out, set a modest personal goal of 500 word count a day; do this every morning (earlier in the day is always better when writing [yes there's uncited science that supports this opinion]). Do this habitually and sequentially as the habit develop; demand of yourself more words per day—you'll know what that upper limit is when you hit it. In the beginning, take the first five consecutive days' copy and on the fifth day compile that 2,500-word copy and start ripping it apart (a.k.a. editing). If you are inferring the use of calendar with committed blocks of time for these tasks, bright girl/boy you are. Your first pass should be reductive with the goal of finding more economical ways of describing/explaining the topic. Your second pass of editing should emphasize points of clarification, often you will know far more than the reader on the topic, so a modest amount of remedial explaining is necessary (added copy); do this without being a pedantic priss. There after your third pass (you didn't think editing was the easy task, did you?) review for voice and meter. I have found it easier to read the copy out loud; if the copy lands awkwardly on the tongue, it means there is narrative tissue missing or the voice is all wrong. Reading copy out loud provides the opportunity to review what is written rather than what you thought you wrote (I have a nasty habit of dropping articles, conjunctions, and a rapturous tendency for run-on sentence and parentheticals). Reading out loud saves me the embarrassment of an editor sending back drafts with a quip "seek medical attention."

As to organization, this precedes writing and in this example is a case of me not following my own advice. Start with a mind map of the topic and drill down to the various didactic questions, issues, data, methods, and whatever. After that visual exercise, weigh the branches of the mind map; which side needs more development/which is more interesting? Decide which side of the map to follow, turn it into outline, and then guess how much copy needs to cover each topic/sub-topic. The outline (table of contents) is not only a reader's finding aid—it's also your production schedule. For the love of God, don't feel the need to start your way from page one; hop and skip through the various sections, writing minimally a topic sentence for each and then dive into the stuff you are more comfortable with. Writing is emotional; booking an early win (getting copy on page) motivates a virtuous cycle of putting the other, less glamourous stuff on the page. You can flesh those sections out later when you are focusing on them. Remember you'll be editing later; in as much as humans don't multi-task well, we are also not very linear and long spells of focus can tap the tank.

As to the remaining micro-skills, our High Lord editor is holding me to word count, I only have the room to briefly stress the importance of follow-through. Lots of people want to be an anthropologist. The ones that have jobs and careers are the ones that not only can do the needed task but do the needed task. Yes, they write. Pick up your reluctant pen and write, only through the sharing of anthropological perspectives and its data shall the public, currently enamored with a celebration of ignorance and easily baited by divisive rhetoric as they are, can be served. And remember "done" is always better than perfect. Perfection is one of those fine notions that is seldom required. Developing the micro-skills on your way to be a Master of the trade, that's a far more tenable objective than perfection. The only one holding you back from that outcome is you—by not doing the necessary sets and reps that get you there.

Some Hidden Facets of Writing Archaeology

Madonna L. Moss

When I was first hired at the University of Oregon, Don Dumond gave one piece of advice: "write like hell." In Darby Stapp's email message of October 2018, he asked a group of us contributors whether there has been a decline in anthropological writing. I believe your answer depends on the type of anthropological writing under consideration. While competition is tight for publication of articles in certain journals, regional journals have experienced declines in submissions, at least in archaeology. There has been a simultaneous steady decline in the publication of archaeological monographs in favor or narrowly focused journal articles. We may also see a decline of edited volumes in the near future, except for those in which the editors are senior graduate students. All these trends are new ways to "play the game" of publishing and are the consequence of pressures in the academy where administrators are most interested in hiring "stars," with over-the-top performance metrics that value international and national outlets over regional journals like *JONA*. In our annual (and other) reviews, faculty are asked to evaluate ourselves on our "research-related output efficiency," which is most easily measured by article counts, journal rankings, and the "h-index." The h-index (Hirsch index) measures the "impact" of an author based on the number of publications that have received h or more citations. As an example, my h-index is currently twenty-six, meaning I have twenty-six publications that have been cited at least twenty-six times. My i10-index is fifty-three, but I admit to having to look up the definition of this index. It means fifty-three of my articles have at least ten citations. Personally, I am appalled that one's academic "output" gets reduced to such numbers. I find such reductionist ways of evaluating one's contributions both insulting and demoralizing.

The most damaging trend of those described above is the decline of the archaeological monograph. Producing a monograph requires leadership, organization, and industriousness. Over the past fifteen or more years, many archaeological sites have been excavated, but the pressure to publish is so intense, that scholars focus on single (and often small) problems that can be addressed relatively quickly in journal article form. They may chip away at the larger analysis, but people seem to have forgotten the long-term value of thorough and complete reporting of archaeological investigations. A concomitant trend is the completion of article-based dissertations instead of monographs. I believe it is our solemn responsibility to report all aspects of an archaeological investigation, and that because monographs present primary data within a holistic context, they have enduring value. Archaeologists have to be trained to be good writers; we owe it to the archaeological record. Good monographs stand the test of time and will be consulted for years to come. Although most monographs won't garner headlines in *National Geographic* or other splashy media outlets, they will be consulted and cited in the future and they are a lasting legacy of our collective investments in recovering archaeological data. Our students who will work in the heritage industry need to know how to document their field projects. These are essential parts of the archaeological record that are not adequately valued in the academic arena today.

I think most of us have experienced a surge in one area of writing: email. Unfortunately, the more responsible you are at answering emails, the more work you generate for yourself. The more you do email, the more email you do. Every week I spend so much more time on email than I would like. My email is perpetually "out-of-control;" I have concluded it is uncontrollable. Although email has facilitated communication among scholars and has (perhaps) hastened the pace of journal article review and publication, I think that we have also witnessed degradation in the tone of scholarly communication. Everyone is under such time pressure, it is easy to be overly blunt; I know I am guilty of this. I recall with great affection thoughtful letters scholars used to write to one another. I still have letters written to me by colleagues R. G. Matson, R. Lee Lyman, Aubrey Cannon, and James Petersen from the 1990s. These were thoughtful and substantive responses to recent publications, and raised important questions for us to consider in future work. These represent the type of scholarly feedback one craves, but rarely receives. They were acts of intellectual generosity that I treasure. I have received few emails that compare in depth or insight.

This brings me to aspects of writing that are even more deeply hidden: the manuscript review process. As a manuscript reviewer, I know I've spent untold hours helping writers clarify their arguments and improve their writing. This work is rarely acknowledged, and sometimes over the years, I've probably spent more time improving an author's writing than they did. This dynamic occurred especially in the first decade after my Ph.D., when I was reviewing works of senior male scholars. On the one hand, I was able to read new and emerging work, on the other hand, I would spend 60+ hours reviewing a book-length manuscript and writing up detailed comments, in some cases, for individuals who had not taken sufficient time to write carefully. In my experience, male and female authors also tend to respond differently to reviewer comments. When I submit something for publication, I almost always comply with suggestions and re-work a ms. following the editor's and reviewers' comments. May I suggest that this is not how male authors always respond; in my experience they are more apt to be defensive and explain why they don't have to pay attention to reviewer comments. This behavior has a clear gendered dimension and may not have been experienced by everyone. I hope that it is changing. Also note that my words "may I suggest" are a feminized figure of speech, intended to soften the edge of my observation. As women, we learn to speak and write this way, sometimes to our detriment. I recall one more senior female scholar admonishing me to "write like you have a penis." This wise woman will remain unnamed here.

Over the years, I have been worried about the under-representation of women authors, particularly when it comes to theoretical work. Consider this: if I were to come up with a new approach to the topic of the initial settlement of the Americas or a new take on the coastal migration theory, am I likely to get it published or cited? I am betting the first attack I would face would be: "where is her evidence?" Yet some male scholars can put together the flimsiest of stories and get them published (sometimes in multiple places). I know that my hypothetical narrative is less likely to get published because I am female. For many women, it is harder to get theoretical work published, and much easier to focus on empirical work that is of undeniable, durable value and is less easily dismissed. I recognize this in my own work and I am more comfortable sticking with the empirical. But doesn't this perpetuate and reproduce the patriarchal structure of our discipline? Of course I have been supported by many male colleagues throughout my career. I am very grateful for their encouragement and advice. If any of you reading this essay have reviewed my submitted work, I extend my sincere appreciation for your efforts.

Dr. Stapp also asked contributors if we could share suggestions with writers. I will close with one recommendation related to writing conference presentations. This is a practice I've followed for years that has always helped me. It is particularly valuable in crafting the fifteen-minute conference paper. I always read my paper aloud, sentence by sentence (multiple times), which allows me to hear all the superfluous words. Then I cut out those words as I aim for clarity and succinctness.

Writing Tensions: Voices That Help—and Those That Don't

Mark S. Warner

Part I: Finding my Voice

Thank you Mike Agar.

In my first semester of graduate school I had a class taught by the cultural anthropologist Mike Agar. In that class he had us read a book he wrote called *The Professional Stranger* (1980). We read the book partway through the semester after I had listened to him lecture in class for a few weeks. What struck me when reading his book was how there were places where I could literally hear his voice while reading. Reading Mike's work was, at times, remarkably like hearing Mike talk. I found that to be a revelation. Up to that point almost all of my school readings had never come across as sounding anything like a class lecture (try reading a typical journal article out loud—see how it sounds). The distinctive parallel between Mike's writing and hearing his voice has periodically come back to me over the years.

I went on from Mike's class and several years later produced a dissertation. Looking back on that not-so-classic work it is full of everything I grumble about today. Overall it is a fairly defensive piece of work, I make an argument and then spend many pages justifying why it was appropriate to use particular data. I also spend pages explaining potential contextual problems as well as preemptively refuting anticipated counter arguments to some of my claims. Years later I was able to clean up some of that writing (primarily through cutting sections) and my 350 page dissertation was turned into a 180 page book. My point here is that sometimes it takes a while to find your voice and have the confidence to write in a way that is comfortable for you rather than writing like you think something should sound.

Now to be honest, I really think that it takes time to find your voice, writing changes in part from simply growing as a professional. Personally I've experienced two things that come with time. The first is that the longer you do something, the more confidence you have in your abilities. Over time, I am increasingly confident in simply stating the positions that I want to take and explaining the rationale/evidence behind my arguments. I stopped worrying about trying to please everyone by anticipating what they *may* want to comment on or critique. The second benefit of time is that the longer you are in a profession you begin to identify people who are somewhat more like you in their writing. You find people like Jim Deetz, Adrian Praetzellis and my colleague Rodney Frey who have actively tried to tell stories through portions their written work. Let me be clear here, *in no way* am I implying that I have anywhere near the rhetorical eloquence of those folks. Rather, I embrace their boldness to write as they want to.

So to return to Mike Agar, when I re-read portions of *Professional Stranger* today there are still portions of that work where I can hear him speaking what I am reading—His writing and speaking came to me as a single voice—My goal is that my writing continues to move in that direction.

(Michael Agar died in May of 2017, as happens all too often, I never got around to reaching back out to Mike to tell him about my impressions of his writing and teaching.)

Part II: Losing my Voice/the Evils of Email

> Darby,
> Apologies for not being clearer about that
> Mark w.

(Full text of an email from Mark Warner sent to Darby Stapp on September 6, 2018. It was one of thirty-three emails I sent that day).

Sharp eyed folks may notice a couple of minor issues in the email—namely that I didn't put a period at the end of the sentence and that I didn't capitalize my last name initial. So I made two punctuation mistakes in ten words. People who are in regular correspondence with me through email will nod their heads knowingly. Frankly my emails are kind of sloppy and I acknowledge some responsibility for that. However, this little vignette is also the tip of a broader and somewhat insidious issue which is that our lives are dominated by expedient forms of communication such as email and/or twitter. On a daily basis we are jotting out quick missives such as my example. The question is what is the impact of this form of writing?

To explore this issue a bit further I went back and tabulated the word count for the 30 emails I actually sent on that day (three were emails I that forwarded on without comment). I wrote 1,327 words in those emails, the longest email consisted of 206 words. Put another way those emails amount to roughly four to five typed pages of work—or a good solid start on an article or book chapter. If you want to be really depressed about your productivity, extrapolate out those numbers over time. At that rate one could have a 200-page manuscript done in about 45 working days!

So what are the impacts? I think there is a corrosive effect on writing when you are slapping out emails all day. Specifically I would note three issues. The first is that "writing" becomes a quick and dirty thing. I end up pounding out emails during fifteen-minute lulls between meetings or while travelling or while waiting for someone, etc. In other words I am repeatedly jotting down responses. The result of just typing and sending is that work becomes a series of (poorly punctuated) snippets/bullet points and, speaking personally, it becomes sloppy. To be clear, there are times where I will spend a day crafting and editing an email before sending it, but what is typical are emails such as the one that opened this section—acknowledge it and move on to the next one in your in box.

A second issue is that a fatigue factor that comes into play. If I spend a big chunk of the day on a computer typing emails in fifteen-minute spurts, by the end of the day I am thoroughly done staring at my computer and typing—particularly since I have also been staring at the same screen working on presentation slides, spread sheets, etc. Physically I need to do something else—a state that doesn't help structured writing at all.

A final, and somewhat related point is that I think email has an impact on the discipline needed to write. As mentioned, I already spend a great deal of time staring at a computer every day. Beyond fatigue I also find that when writing almost anything these days I am readily distracted by incoming email pop ups (I know I can turn that off) or anticipating a time sensitive response to an email. I bang out emails all day but I now struggle to sit down and write 500 words in a dedicated block of time. My pop psychology diagnosis is email-induced attention deficit issues.

A final caveat: I am somewhat of a technological Luddite, I am on email, but I do not have Facebook, Twitter, or Instagram accounts. Email and all of these other social media platforms have absolutely transformed our ability to keep in touch and readily communicate with many, many people. In many regards that is a huge positive for the workplace. However I also think that a world increasingly consumed by staccato writing is not a world that fosters the creation of eloquent prose.

WHY DON'T WE WRITE MORE?

From Writing Science to Writing for the General Public

Dennis Dauble

During my thirty-five-year career as a fisheries scientist, I wrote over one hundred fifty peer-reviewed articles and technical reports. I did so both because I learned the craft, and because it was a requirement for my profession. I have continued to write during retirement because, to paraphrase what Robert Barrass wrote in his self-help book, *Scientists Must Write*, "Writing helps you remember, helps you observe, and helps you think." One difference is that I no longer sit down at my computer to describe the results of laboratory or field studies. Instead, my current interest focuses on writing for the general public.

There are discrete differences in the two genres. For example, the organization of a typical scientific article is more prescriptive. The introduction includes a problem statement and a review of related literature. A methods section that follows is basically a description of what and how. Results include summary tables and figures along with explanatory narrative text. The final section or Discussion is the most important. Inference is drawn from key results and summary thinking is backed up with citations from the scientific literature.

Similar to a scientific article, narrative non-fiction requires a theme or a thread that takes the reader through the story from beginning to end. What's different though, is non-fiction authors have more opportunity to opine or wax poetic. Emotions can be bared; conversation revealed. One step further down the literary trail takes authors into creative non-fiction, an emerging genre that allows you to embellish facts "for the sake of story."

My current business card reads, "scientist, writer, educator." I chose those words carefully. Along with consulting on contemporary fisheries issues, I am a Board member of the Northwest Outdoor Writing Association, and I speak to conservation groups on such topics as the impacts of dams to salmon, bird-fish interactions, and the history of fish and fishing. These public interactions reinforce the importance of me being able to relate to an audience, especially when the goal is to educate them on a scientific topic.

According to the Oxford Dictionary, *journal* means a logbook, daily record, or diary. One thing I learned as a practicing scientist was the importance of maintaining data and formal observations in a logbook. I relied on logbooks (often with a quality assurance manual by my side) to record field and laboratory observations. These records served the basis for later scientific articles and reports. In contrast, my current collection of field journals capture details of outdoor adventure. For example, I might record the condition of weather, stream flow, phenology of native plants, wildlife observed, geological landscapes, fish caught (or lost), and whatever else comes to mind.

I keep a leather-bound journal beside my bed, write-in-the-rain notebooks in my truck and boat, and a pocket journal in every jacket and vest I take into the field. Over the past several decades, this habit has led to a pile of mismatched journals stored under lock and key in my den. Some evenings, I pull a journal from the bookcase and am reminded of poignant moments. Like the frosty autumn morning when my son caught his first trout, the camping trip when I accidentally broke wife Nancy's ankle while busting up firewood, and the August night when I woke to the scream of a cougar while a full moon rose over the Blue Mountains.

But more important, journaling provides fodder for non-fiction magazine articles and books that I write. The process of taking detailed notes allows me to capture the moment, tie down fleeting thoughts, and attach images to a time and place. I also record conversation that would otherwise be impossible to recreate. In this manner, my journals serve as a logbook of activities, settings, and feelings that would otherwise be lost.

In 2009, I wrote a natural history guidebook for people who wanted to know more about fish. I incorporated what I learned as a practicing scientist, classroom teacher, and avid angler. It wasn't easy. I studied writing aids, worked on my grammar, and developed a more consistent voice. These same writing skills might come natural to someone with a Masters Degree in Fine Arts, but not when you have a Ph.D. in a science discipline.

There are similarities in my previous and current writing life. For example, careful introspection and rigorous peer review are essential. Reading within and outside of my area of expertise continues to be important. Meeting deadlines and managing word count come into play, as does making friends with editors. I strive to include science in my stories whenever possible through the use of historical and life history facts. Admittedly, eliminating scientific jargon can be a challenge. Much like writing for other scientists though, writing for the general public is all about story. Tell a good story and you can communicate with any audience.

ESSAYS ON WRITING AND PUBLISHING

Part 3

Part 3 contains the following essays:

- "A Commentary on Publishing" by Bruce Granville Miller, Professor, Department of Anthropology, University of British Columbia, and Canadian Anthropology Society Fellow. Miller's research concerns Indigenous peoples and their relations with the state in its various local, national, and international manifestations. Miller has authored or edited eight books and some two hundred journal articles, chapters, and reviews.
- "Why Write" by Jay Miller, an anthropologist in the old-school Americanist tradition, rescuing, researching, sharing, and writing about cultural contexts, archaeology, history, beliefs, kinship, lifeways, and languages of the Indigenous peoples across North America. Miller has written or edited fifty-five books and one hundred twenty articles.
- "Unearth and Heft" by Nathaniel D. Reynolds, an ethnoecologist and Interim Cultural Program Manager with the Cowlitz Indian Tribe. He received a M.S. in Environmental Science and Regional Planning in 2009 from the Vancouver Branch Campus of Washington State University.
- "The Language of Writing" by Astrida R. Blukis Onat, an archaeologist and ethnographer who received a Ph.D. in Anthropology from Washington State University in 1980; taught anthropology at Seattle Central Community College for 27 years; and founded BOAS, Inc., a CRM firm, in 1982. She has authored and coauthored more than 30 major data recovery investigations and monographs, more than a dozen published papers, three short archaeology teaching films, several brochures about archaeological sites, and too many CRM reports to enumerate. For the past 30 years, she has worked with certain tribes conducting ethnographic research for legal proceeding.
- "The Tin Shed: Why I Write" by Rodney Frey, Professor Emeritus in Ethnography at the University of Idaho, having received his Ph.D. in Anthropology from the University of Colorado in 1979. He has conducted collaborative, applied ethnographic projects with the Crow, Coeur d'Alene, Nez Perce, Warm Springs and Wasco Tribes, among

others. Of primary concern has been the role and the significance of oral traditions, particularly as those traditions influence a people's relationships with their "landscape" and mediate the impact of Euro-American influences. As collaborative projects, he has also been concerned with the ethical issues associated with Tribal sovereignty and cultural property rights. Frey has authored five books, four internet books, five journal articles, and six book chapters.

A Commentary on Publishing

Bruce Granville Miller

My first anthropology publication came with the help and guidance of my dissertation supervisor at Arizona State University, Brian Foster. He had an insight into the work I was doing regarding Coast Salish social networks that I couldn't yet see; he showed me how I might mathematically operationalize concepts used metaphorically by Suttles and Elmendorf. That same year I published a piece about the federal recognition project, an interest I developed while working with the then-unrecognized Samish tribe. I noticed that not much was being written about an important, largely invisible process. I fell into both of these publications.

My first thought, then, is that instructors and professors should help students to develop some small, interesting corner of their thesis or dissertation research projects that might make a tight, engaging paper. This worked for me with Tad McIlwraith, now a professor at Guelph, and what I think was his first publication. This concerned the movement of Plains/Prairie ritual practices into the Coast Salish territories. We talked about this while he was a student in my ethnographic fieldschool run with the Stó:lô Nation. We were living in a longhouse in Chilliwack and a ritual leader there told us of his dismay about the use of tobacco. Tad used it as an opportunity to write about ideas of culture, responses to the contemporary world, and other issues which were of interest beyond the longhouse. On another occasion a graduate student I supervised gave a talk to a small departmental audience. Listening, I recognized a very strong insight into the issue of Israeli immigration to Vancouver. Just as in my own case, he hadn't yet realized, but it soon produced a nice publication.

Students at UBC ask where they might publish something and what the publication process is about. I spend time in a graduate pro-seminar on this and typically students don't know much about it. I go over nuts and bolts—reading journal guidelines, the length of time before they might inquire if there is progress on reviewing their paper, the sorts of responses they might get and how to reply (promptly, I tell them, before the editor changes his or her mind). I suggest that they lose their inhibitions and fears about publishing and recognize that even at the M.A. stage, most of them have something to say. They don't quite realize that. Part of this might be called finding your voice.

There are different stages in creating a writing career. A significant difficulty that I had early on was realizing when to stop in a paper and not to cram too many issues into too little space. An editor wrote in response to an early submission that the reviewers liked it, but there was too much content. I am thankful to those people for the good advice; I divided the paper in half and got two publications out of it. Eventually I learned to write papers which fit both my interests and the formats of particular journals. A few years later I published my first book, *The Problem of Justice*, which concerns Coast Salish historic practices and their responses to colonization. The Stó:lô Nation leadership had asked if I would do some background research on their justice practices. In the course of interviewing a Vancouver Island chief, I had the sudden realization that what he was telling me about their ancestral practices was significantly different than what I was told by Coast Salish leaders in Puget Sound and on the Fraser River. I realized on the spot that this must reflect differences in contact history and public policy aimed at Indigenous peoples. *That is a book*, I thought right then. A lot of publishing is about the unexpected.

My own approach is to write about things that matter in the present-day world. With few exceptions, the ideas come from the Indigenous communities with which I work. For example, I have worked with several non-recognized tribes and bands and found that there was no world-wide review of why there were so many of these groups. I came to realize that just as Indigenous populations were growing world-wide, resource extract was occurring in marginal locations where the Indigenous peoples had been pushed. Many countries came up with ways to administratively erase them and I wrote the first world examination of the issue. This arose initially from my work with the Samish. I fell into this, too. I didn't set out to do this.

I can't separate my writing philosophy from my research approach. More generally, my research strategy is to get inside the playing out of a social controversy, see it from the perspective of participants and write about it. Strangely, this seems to be an unusual practice. Here is an example: some years ago, an attorney contacted me to see if I could would provide expert testimony regarding the case of a First Nations woman harassed by security guards in a downtown mall. I thought about this and tried to write about the long-term adverse effects of surveillance and racialized segregation in Vancouver on Indigenous people now. This resulted in my testimony in *Radek* in the BC Human Rights Tribunal, testimony since cited by the Supreme Court. More of our students today are working on real-world issues and, I think, ought to write about them from the inside. Real issues identified from the ground up make good research programs and publications. These generally come from the application of very basic anthropology, such as how kinship and exchange systems work.

The next point about writing again concerns research methods: our students in anthropology are taught formal research methods and go through elaborate human subjects protocols as part of their graduate training. They learn, then, about creating one-off, complex research agendas, the results of which become thick dissertations. I did this, too, to get a doctorate. But I rarely do anything like that now. More likely, I am involved in small-scale events or productions which, taken together, provide the material for journal publications. It is the old bricolage approach once familiar to anthropology and memorialized by Lévi-Strauss. More publications might result if anthropologists were alive to the various things they have learned, just by living, watching, and participating in, as in my case, the Coast Salish world. This is a form of generalist practice which, I think, is well suited to the anthropology of today. A great example is a recent *Current Anthropology* paper by Bill Angelbeck, John Welch, Dave Schaepe and others, about understanding the therapeutic effects of engaging in archaeology for Indigenous community members.

A book I wrote, *Oral History on Trial*, emerged after I was goaded into giving expert testimony about the use of oral history evidence in Canada by the crown expert, following a Supreme Court decision which gave oral history the "same footing as written history." Here, the challenge of writing a book about all of this was sharing space with people with a strong sense of the importance of their discipline. In my case, this was legal scholars. My strategy was to ask some retired judges to explain legal concepts and to respond to ideas I had about how oral history evidence could be used. It worked. People like to explain their fields, I find, and we might seek out more allies and collaborators as a way to get into print and to take advantage of our discipline's rare groundedness. Part of my point here is that our students may not fully appreciate how distinct a grounded perspective is, and how valuable it is to our contemporary society, which is generally studied from above, in the abstract, and divorced from living people. I am struck by the frequency with which I hear ideas graduate students have which should be developed into journal submissions. To *JONA*, in many cases.

In brief, senior anthropologists might help students find the message in their own work and in community identified projects, and encourage them to submit to journals. I'm sure many do this already. We can inform them about the publishing process and how to work with it. We can point out journals for them to consider. And, we can encourage them to look beyond large scale projects to assembling the smaller bits of knowledge they gain as they go along. In addition, we can encourage participation in team publications and in projects with real connection to current social problems, and to embrace the unexpected. Above all, we can help our students understand that our disciplinary approach of looking at issues from the ground up is distinctive and valuable and worth writing about. Nobody else is doing it, and nobody will, if we and they don't.

ESSAYS ON WRITING AND PUBLISHING

Why Write

Jay Miller

As a second generation Boasian, the eternal importance of write up was instilled in me repeatedly. This was further reinforced when I tried to find reports of important archaeological excavations in the Southwest for my own Ph.D. only to end in the disappointing realization there were neither notes nor final write ups of crucial sites. Often the only source of any information at all came informally in bars over drinks, often many of them to loosen tongues and long buried memories.

Finally, technology began to provide another solution as timing, people, place, and growing annoyance with a shirking profession glibly denying our ancestors; all converged to urge me toward self-publish my dozen long-languishing book drafts based on intensive work with key knowledge-holding elders, making them widely and readily available to tribes and scholars who have been so very helpful over the years and deserve to have their contributions on record. Following Smithsonian recommendations for the Handbook, these works are intended to be standard references for fifty years out.

Approaching her 100th birthday in 2016, Amelia Susman Schultz (Columbia Anthropological Linguistics Ph.D. 1939, chaired by Franz Boas) wanted more brain stimulation to accompany her regular tai chi and yoga and was told that "proof reading" was among the best mental challenges. She began by asking several friends and colleagues if they had manuscripts for her to work on, and, approaching me, I was only too happy to oblige with something I knew would interest her, bringing her abreast of Americanists decades on. After her requisite three reviews—for obvious typos and mistakes, for grammar, and for sense—of each manuscript, she returned a superbly corrected copy. Others soon followed, though she is always urged to keep to her own pace.

Of note, Amelia wrote two dissertations, one on acculturation at Round Valley that she was asked to withdraw so seven of her peers could get their Ph.D.s with the publication of a book featuring chapters that were their dissertations. Her second was a grammar featuring Aspect in Ho-Chunk ~ Winnebago, with the famous Crashing Thunder Sam Blowsnake, Big Ho-Chunk as her native speaker, approved in 1939, but not published until she used her first paycheck as a WWII WAC to make off-set printed copies that she sent to libraries and department to finally qualify for an awarded Ph.D. in 1943. Indeed, publication counted from the very beginning for Boasians.

The *Journal of Northwest Anthropology* (*JONA*), where I am associate editor, shifted in 2015 to Amazon self-publishing for its journal issues and memoirs, including a collection (*Memoir* 9) of twenty-five of my own articles. This shift introduced me to the digital procedure as well as provided me with hands-on guidance as I began publishing my own works and improving my CreateSpace skills. Near the end of 2018, CreateSpace was moved over to Kindle, where my paperback and E-books reside for sale on Amazon.

Another precipitating factor was the review and acceptance of an earlier manuscript by the academic press that has published several of my other volumes. This time, however, my Mounds draft was cut in half, and the reviewers (some my friends) were less than helpful, if not overly caustic and clueless. Self-publishing sidesteps these personal difficulties and preserves otherwise fraught friendships. In part, their startled reactions derive from my own limited participation in academic conferences, where my progressing analysis of data was expected to be marshaled and interpreted so as to be vetted in public during the solitary writing-up process.

Along with these ongoing pressures and traumas, are factors of aging. Medical concerns arose that urged quick action, carrying me through awkward and frustrating misadventures with computers, programs, texts, and PDFs.

As an active reader, I have also benefited from interviews with professionals. P. D. James taught me to write about what I am most interested on that day and then weave together the many pieces at the very end, writing the beginning overview at the very end. Tony Hillerman taught persistence in pursuit of publication, even as he was repeatedly told to leave out the Indians by earlier reviewers of his Navajo series. Many other writers have since woven ethnic themes and peoples into series now popular in the US, Canada, and internationally.

Focusing on outcomes, distractions and conflicts were held off as I concentrated more and more on final edits, revisions, and hard copies. While time and money have usually been mutually exclusive for me, I suddenly had a bit of both, as more and more scholars espoused "digital humanities" despite incongruence within Indien country, where electricity can be beyond the means of families and native churches still rely on candlelight.

Finally, by making quantities of my books readily available to native families fulfills mutual pledges with scholarly elders, spanning decades, half a century in cases. Thus, my life burdens are lifting and my future options include more freedoms, sharing, promise, and flexibility among wider choices.

Unearth and Heft

Nathaniel D. Reynolds

An invitation by *JONA's* editors to contribute an essay to a volume on anthropological writing is an unexpected honor, especially because I never set out to do anthropology—I stumbled into the field by luck and happenstance. Instead, my education, field training, and personal interests focused on natural history and ecological conservation. I came to science as a memorizer, able to recall Latin names and obscure facts. Picture the classic Scottish naturalist collecting and preserving specimens, preparing them for shipping from some distant shore back to the halls of Edinburgh. These were my heroes, and their tools were fieldbooks of jotted notes and Victorian-era curiosity cabinets packed with artifacts, fossils, and oddities. I was dismayed during the early stages of my master's thesis research to learn that making species lists and recognizing patterns was no longer *de rigeur*. I was told: "No, you'll need to find a project where you can look at pattern, hypothesize what process causes the pattern, then test the hypothesis to determine whether or not your beliefs about the process are valid. We kick the tires these days!"

Twelve years ago, I was hired by the Cowlitz Indian Tribe to work in their Natural Resources Department. I focused on conserving and restoring species and habitats that are culturally-relevant to the Cowlitz People. I assembled long lists of ethnobotanical references, and learned the names of places in the landscape that are traditional resource-gathering sites. I apprenticed with Cowlitz knowledge, learning how to roast camas roots in an earth oven, how to dip and smoke-dry eulachon, what season is right for pulling cedar bark. I swung stone adzes and hefted fishing weights unearthed from archaeological sites. In the discipline of anthropology (in a comparative sense to ecology) these details are pattern.

Old-style anthropology, like old-style natural history, often emphasizes artifacts and cultural materials. But these items no more adequately represent a living culture than a moth-eaten, taxidermied museum wolf represents its lithe, wise, and fierce incarnation. Heritage items of material culture are silent and asleep in glass museum cases.

They come alive when they are talked to, honored, used, and put into a cultural context, but only by the people who made them, loved them, and lived with them for generations.

I recently toured the American Museum of Natural History in New York, and the Northwest Coast Hall (opened in 1899 under direction of Franz Boaz, the "father of American anthropology") is getting a prominent update. On October 15th, 2018, the museum announced the appointment of *Nuu-chah-nulth* artist and cultural historian *Haa'yuups* (Ron Hamilton) as co-curator for the redeveloping Northwest Coast Hall.

In the press release announcing the appointment, Peter Whiteley, the museum's curator of North American Ethnology, stated: "With the reimagining of the Hall, our goal is to present the art and material culture of the Pacific Northwest in a way that highlights the ideas, voices, and perspectives past and present behind these wonderful historical pieces." Museum President Ellen V. Futter observed: "*Haa'yuups* will bring an important perspective for millions from all over the world who will visit the reimagined Northwest Coast Hall and its updated presentation of cultural treasures."[1]

This opportunity to give some space and voice to the dynamic, living culture, the processual agent, the cause of the artifacts and art-effects, is progress! But the language of the museum representatives still primarily focuses on the trappings of culture, the glass cabinets commodifying "wonderful historical pieces" and "cultural treasures," rather than putting the rich political, cultural, and social identities of the makers foremost.

The discipline of anthropology, like ecology, is slowly learning it is an error to pit process versus pattern. Rather, process and pattern (like cause and effect) are a dualism. They complement, inform, and rely on each other, and can best be understood in an integrated, holistic way. In ecology, the route to understanding process begins with recognizing and describing pattern; effective anthropological analysis likewise should proximally begin with pattern, but ultimately illuminate the meaning of culture and identity, and be reported in a

---

[1] https://www.amnh.org/about-the-museum/press-center/haa-yuups-renowned-nuu-chah-nulth-artist-and-cultural-historian-named-co-curator-in-restoration-of-historic-northwest-coast-hall

hybrid and intersectional manner. The objects alone cannot speak, and the tenacious people who made them are the ones who testify best to the heritage of use, of the cultural meaning imbued in the physical material.

Nazarea[2] introduces ethnoecology as "a way of looking at the relationship between humans and the natural world" including the cultural "schema, scripts and plans that orient people," and yes, looking is good. But listening may be even better. I believe a successful path to understanding Indigenous ways of being—or perceiving what knowing and living with non-dominant cultural heritage means in our modern world—is to directly hear the voices of the Indigenous in the narrative.

My philosophy of writing, my "always a beginner" entry to Indigenous process/pattern dualism, is this query: "What does it mean to be Cowlitz, in this time and place?" I ask Cowlitz citizens endless, bothersome questions: What does it mean to the Cowlitz that mountain goats are returning to the slopes of Mount St. Helens/*Lawetlat'la*? What does it mean for Cowlitz identity that eulachon population numbers are low? What does the act of digging camas roots mean for you? What do you feel when you hear your great-grandmother, her voice recorded on a wax cylinder, sing her huckleberry-picking song? I record their answers and file them away in the Cowlitz Tribal Archives. They speak their own words. I only listen.

I adopt this approach in my writing, and recently co-authored a *JONA* article titled "The Pacific Crabapple and Cowlitz Cultural Resurgence."[3] The first half of the article presented pattern: a review of crabapple harvest and processing techniques along the Northwest Coast. The second half of the article detailed a modern Cowlitz crabapple harvest. It explored what it means for resurgent Cowlitz identity and Cowlitz People to be doing the act of harvest, at this time, in that place. Christine Dupres, co-author and Cowlitz citizen, was fundamental in expressing opinions and Indigenous frames of thought that I, as a white researcher, cannot fully know. When we sent an initial draft out for review and comment, one editor commented, "This first part is fascinating, but the lengthy section about Cowlitz identity at

---

[2] Nazarea VD, 1999, Preface, in *Nazarea VD (Ed.) Ethnoecology: Situated Knowledge/Located Lives*. University of Arizona Press, Tucson AZ, USA

[3] Reynolds ND and Dupres C, 2018. The Pacific Crabapple (*Malus fusca*) and Cowlitz Cultural Resurgence, *Journal of Northwest Anthropology*, Vol 52(1):36–62.

the end should be significantly reduced." Another editor said, "Remove all this dry ethnographic first part and focus on Cowlitz identity. That's where the paper really happens." In the end, we tightened and kept both sections—and let process and pattern, cause and effect, entwine on the page.

This is my approach to writing anthropology. I strive to find compelling perspectives—to unearth and heft meaning in the material. Then I ask pattern and process to dance with each other in order to more closely express the through-line and truth of the narrative. And as much as possible, I try to get out of the way so the voices of the People themselves come through.

WHY DON'T WE WRITE MORE?

The Language of Writing

Astrida R. Blukis Onat

The following essay contains personal experiences with learning language, considers structural elements of writing, and suggests the extent to which writing is culturally circumscribed. It is a reflection of a lifetime trying to write in English.

As a child, one is not aware of just how much is learned very early about using language. Accents, idioms, and metaphors that float in adult conversations are picked up as children grow. Children's books tell cultural stories. These bits of communication will be used in speaking and writing in later years. A child placed in situations where multiple languages are being spoken may absorb all of them simultaneously and master the particulars of each as they grow up. They can code switch at will, and will continue to do that as adults. They will be truly bilingual and bicultural. If childhood languages are learned sequentially, confusion may result. As a new language and culture displaces the old, each will be known incompletely. English was the fourth language I learned before the age of ten.

My first languages, Latvian and Russian, were learned simultaneously. At age four, my family left Latvia for Germany. Russian was left behind. Living in Germany for the next five years, I learned to speak German and spoke it fluently from ages four to nine. We continued to speak Latvian with parents and in our refugee community. When I was nine, we emigrated to the US. At home, we continued to speak Latvian. Since there was little opportunity to speak Latvian outside a family context, I never managed to become truly articulate in adult Latvian.

By the time I finished high school, English was my major language. My fantasies of being a good writer were frustrated for lack of the basic elements of a language most children learn as they grow up. What I call the "story bits," were missing. The best I could do was follow the rules of grammar and attack writing assignments with correct spelling. It became clear that my writing would be limited to term papers, theses, and a dissertation in the social and natural sciences.

The structure of Euro-American writing is linear, with a beginning, a middle, and an end. Scholarly writing begins with an argument, provides data, and ends with a conclusion. A personal voice is missing and not encouraged. Because such writing is meant for a limited audience of fellow professionals, writing can be full of professional jargon—a sub-language. Conclusions are hesitant and couched in equivocating clauses. The language used is specialized and is not understood by the general public. I have written many cultural resource reports and authored papers within this structure.

Midway through my archaeological career, I conducted research in post-Soviet Latvia. I found that Latvian archaeologists used ethnographic and historic data to both search for archaeological sites and to interpret what was discovered. "Story" was a part of this research and writing. Given this model, I determined to use local ethnographic studies to address investigations in the Puget Sound area, become more informed regarding contemporary tribal culture, and include both in my interpretation of regional archaeology.

The earliest ethnographers spoke to tribal people at a time when an older generation of native speakers was being lost. The ethnographers all made some effort to learn the native language. The next generation of native Lushootseed speakers learned the language from their parents, meanwhile learning English outside the home and in school. These bilingual persons often translated for their elders. Information was recorded mostly in English.

My first serious attempt to incorporate tribal story with archaeological data came in an unfortunate context. We were conducting an archaeological survey of an area associated with a geologically unique rock promontory. Adjacent to the promontory, we found a petroglyph showing two snakes carved into a large boulder. An archaeological site also was located nearby. The owner of the property wanted to mine it for the rock and was intent on determining that associated archaeological materials were not important. The Upper Skagit Tribe was trying to preserve the feature because of its cultural significance. In preparing for a legal hearing, we gathered ethnographic information about the location to support the archaeological data.

In a Nookachamps story anchored in this landscape, the promontory is identified as Snake. Two other rock features in the floodplain on the small river are named Mouse and Frog. Another character, Beaver, also is featured. He lives in Beaver Lake nearby and has his own house. Two versions of the story had been documented in the 1950s.[1] The two pages of the story describe the natural environment, give details of the effects of major flooding, and include a humorous discussion of marriage customs as represented by the animal actors. Features of the landscape are used to structure the story. The connections between the story, the archaeology, and the place were very obvious in this context.

However, explaining the importance of the rock promontory to non-Indian people with an agenda that was focused only on removing the promontory for profit was an exercise in disconnected communication. Telling the story of Snake had no effect at the hearing. The story was dismissed as "just a myth" and had nothing to do with the promontory. There were no cultural bridges that could be crossed, even with a common language. Snakes, mice, frogs, and rocks were of no importance. Neither was the spiritual significance of geologic remnants. In fact, it seemed that bringing the story into the process made it harder to validate the archaeological finds. The petroglyph was disfigured, the archaeological site ignored, and the promontory has been mined down to a nub. I could not understand why the obvious connection of story to place was so vigorously dismissed, even by some in the archaeological community.

Therefore, I delved ever more deeply into the ethnographic record. I examined the wealth of field notes made by individual ethnographers. Most notes were direct quotes from tribal participants, sometimes backed by audiotapes. From these, it was evident that the information as spoken and written down was structured not at all like how it was presented in publications. The notes revealed the accustomed tribal story form. They were teachings tied to features of the landscape. As such, the notes contained much more information than what was summarized in any publication. Even while providing information about cultures not our own, the academic writing style was structuring interpretation for non-Indians. It was difficult to hear Indian voices in that context.

Perhaps an entire book written from a bicultural perspective would communicate better. Two tribal elders I knew had retired from

---

[1] Snyder, Sally
2002   sgʷaʔčəɬ syəyəhub *Our Stories, Skagit Myths and Tales Collected and Edited by Sally Snyder.* Lushootseed Press, Washington.

tribal work and were assembling a number of stories they had written into a book. Edith Bedal had served as tribal historian and recording secretary during the time the Sauk-Suiattle Tribe was acknowledged, Jean Bedal Fish was tribal Chairman. The mother of the sisters, Susan Wawetkin, was Indian; and their father James Bedal was a pioneer. The sisters spoke the native dialect of the Sauk people, learned from their mother and their Indian relations. The sisters learned to speak English from their father and pioneer neighbors. They learned to write in a school established at the Bedal homestead. The sisters grew up bicultural and bilingual.

Both sisters had written about the tribal history they were a part of. They wrote down the customs and legends as told by their mother. Edith Bedal also wrote about experiences living at the homestead and working as a guide in the mountains around Glacier Peak. Jean Bedal Fish wrote about the early pioneer history of the upper Sauk and Stillaguamish River area. She supplemented her own knowledge with information in early history books, often using phrasing dating to that time. The mix of Sauk legends, family history, tribal history and pioneer history was told in a series of stories. The Sauk River valley was described as a beloved place and the persons who had lived there were endlessly fascinating.

With support from a USFS grant, we organized the writings and selected photographs. I copy edited the stories and wrote a preface. Before they passed away, I promised to get the book published.[2] *Two Voices* was first privately printed in 2000 for a memorial service that included the sisters and other tribal elders.

When I approached three different publishers with the first printing, I was told that the stories could not be published as presented, that the writing style of the Indian legends and that of the historic information was too disparate, and that the collection of stories needed a "context." In other words, the book could not stand on its own and the work needed some explanation. I was somewhat taken aback at this response. The book made total sense to me as I was by then more familiar with tribal customs, local history, and the Sauk area. We even conducted an archaeological excavation at the Bedal homestead. There continued to be demand for this book in Indian country, in the local

---

[2] Edith Bedal (1903–1995); Jean Bedal Fish (1907–1997).

community, and among a few researchers, so extra printings were made, the last of which was published with a new preface in 2016.³

Presently, I am attempting to write the "context" book to go around the stories told in *Two Voices*. I cannot change the nature of the original. I have gathered more information about the area, local history, and the family. I have found more stories and photographs in the materials the sisters left in my care.⁴ The writing structure will be familiar to scholars, with lots of references to *Two Voices*, the information amplified by voluminous footnotes.

The essence of *Two Voices* for me was that the authors wrote in disparate styles but with one focus, telling the story of their homeland and its inhabitants, hence the title. It was clear that they held both the Sauk Indian and the Pioneer perspectives in their beings. They did not try to explain one in terms of the other. The sisters grew up knowing two cultures. They learned local pioneer history, written in linear English. They also wrote down their oral history as they had heard it. They code switched as needed.

Writing the history of a landscape and a people in a written language that is not structured for the task is difficult at best. How does one use a linear structure to present stratified and diffuse information about a homeland full of personal history spanning millennia? There is no beginning or end to the Sauk stories for those accustomed to hearing them in the context of the landscape that is a homeland. Rocks, hillsides, peaks, stream, and rivers tell the story of a people whose ancestors have lived among them. Legends tell of the relationships among people, land, and animals through metaphor. The natural and spiritual world are connected. Social interactions are carried out by the living and non-living. Daily life and work are memorialized in rock promontories. Stories connect to other places and people. Traditional family areas have a local history, the telling of which belongs to people who have remember their experiences in reference to the landscape. It is the setting of the story that structures other elements. That is how

---

³ Fish, Jean Bedal and Edith Bedal
2016   *Two Voices, a History of the Sauk and Suiattle People and Sauk Country Experiences.* BOAS, Inc. Seattle.

⁴ The Bedal materials are slated go the Special Collections at UW once I have finished cataloging them.

the stories in *Two Voices* were written. One could assemble them in any order and pick out one or another as wanted.

And so, I do not have a structured ending for this essay. I cannot reconcile the way the English language is used in scholarship with the way it is structured to tell the old Indian stories. Nor do I feel it is necessary. It is possible to hold both in the heart and see the world from more than one direction. I can read that Snake is a tall guy with grey eyes and stinks and know that the greywacke stone from the promontory has been found in many archaeological sites in the region. I know that when South Wind and North Wind are fighting, there will be toppled trees and the weatherman will tell of dramatic changes in atmospheric pressure. I can see that Tahoma is the mother of all waters and understand that if the ice all melts our rivers will go away. I like to hear the context of a story as told by the original inhabitants. Organizing data to end with a conclusion about an idea is also satisfying. Communicating between these approaches may be difficult but the effort is so very rewarding.

The Tin Shed: Why I Write

Rodney Frey

The following is a compilation of actual events and experiences, chronologically rearranged, to create a personal essay in narrative form. It's a story that seeks to address some perennial questions, through the lens of ethnography. What motivates me to write and what's the philosophy behind that writing? What challenges have I had in getting published? What suggestions do I have for would-be writers? In this storytelling the "answers" are often implicitly embedded in the narrative, many rephrased as questions that can help guide.

I'd arrived early that hot June day, anxious to get started. The interviewee, a Tribal elder of some fifty years my senior, asked if I'd wait on an old wooden bench under the shade of a cottonwood just out front of his modest home. He had a few chores he wanted to first finish. As I sat there, fidgeting with my cassette tape-recorder, going over my many questions, my mind kept wondering, reflecting on just how this urban, middleclass, white-guy, who had a pretty easy upbringing, got to this place. What did I ultimately seek, and why? How would I begin to convey to others what I might learn from this elder? The reflections went beyond simply that I was here now, having been invited by the Tribe, to research what could be done to improve health care delivery.

In the rush of seemingly random thoughts, one stood out. I'd gone to an inner-city high school, with a graduating class of some 800, a quarter of whom were African-American, with significant numbers of Asian-American and Hispanic students. It was a wondrous mix of stories, in the classroom, throughout our community, and on the track. I was a runner, and for this "white boy," pretty good, a member of our state-champion track team. My senior year I anchored our mile relay. We traveled together to meets throughout the state, practiced hard and depended upon each other. Together, we endured disappointments and celebrated accomplishments, together we told stories. I had a sense even then, though not fully comprehending it, that at the core of our humanity, we're all storytellers—*Homo narrans*. On this predominately Black-team, I participated in difference, yet in those fluid moments as the baton was handed off, there was no difference, and in the stories we told, it made all the difference. And I waited for the Native elder.

With the recorder on, I asked about kinship, ceremonies, language, bombarding him with youthful enthusiasm. After a while, enough was enough, and the elder held out his hand, stopping me in mid-sentence. Silence. Then he pointed to a corrugated-metal building, some fifty yards to the north. It housed highway equipment, trucks and tractors, or so I imagined. And turning directly to me, he asked, "Do *you see* that tin shed?...it's kinda like our way of life...you can sit back here and talk about it...but *not really understand*...it's not 'til you get off your bench....go *inside...listen...feel it*...feel it with your *heart*... see it from the *inside* looking out...that you really know what it's all about...you've *gotta go inside*." Later he added, "And I'll come along... *with you*...be with you," and then asked, "What are you *gonna do* with what you've learned?"

There could be no better questions asked, no better preparations offered to a neophyte ethnographer. This little story would guide my journey over the next four decades, as I and my students engaged with the Apsáalooke, the Niimíipuu, the Schitsu'umsh, along with other Native communities. Their stories rich with diversity yet imbued with shared humanity. And in their re-telling, hopefully a difference could be made.

"Do *you see* that tin shed?" The elder could have gotten up, terminating the interview. Instead, he offered a sort of permission, as a host, to engage. It illustrated the critical role in acknowledging Tribal sovereignty and the cultural property rights of your host, and of following the Tribe's research protocols. Would I be invited, as a guest? And I act as one? Would I adhere to a Tribal review of the concluding research, that assessed its authenticity and appropriateness, before going public? Of course, a Tribe might deny permission, deeming a proposal unsuitable, or having their own ethnographer, no need for a guest.

"I'll come along...*with you*." Would I work in collaboration with my host, he a guide, showing the way, and I willing to follow, avoiding mis-steps? Would I become a trusted ally? It's a collaboration from the start, beginning with the research design, continuing as we interviewed, coded, interpreted and formatted the final paper, concluding in co-authorship. None of my annual evaluations or promotion and tenure reviews were ever weakened because of co-authorships, just the contrary. While seemingly trite, isn't research and publication ultimately about respect, relationship and reciprocity, as we *together* explore our differences and reveal our common humanity? And challenging it, a growing essentialism?

"Get off your bench....go *inside...listen...feel* it with your *heart... see it* from the *inside* looking out." If I was to "*listen*" and "*feel*," I mustn't view from afar, but with empathy and my best ethnographic skills, experientially engage in relationships with members of my host community. Relationships built on trust and respect. But even then, perhaps the greatest challenge is in attempting to "*see*" and "*feel*" from the perspective of those I engaged. While ultimately an impossibility, the journey to an "insider's" perspective is nevertheless essential, for the alternative is to continue in ignorance, bias and prejudice. Can I begin to "*feel*" "heart knowing," what the Schitsu'umsh call *hnkhwelkhwlnet*, "our ways of life in the world,"—Indigenous ontology and epistemology? Could I begin to grasp a world view so completely alien to my upbringing? Let go of how I've been taught, replacing it with an Indigenous pedagogy? Let go of my own preconceptions about the nature of reality. Let go of Cartesian Dualism and Aristotelian Materialism, replacing it with the "transitory intersection of those participating—human, animal, plant and spirit peoples—anchored to place-based teachings?" A reality not of discrete objects, reducible to material forms, but of unfolding events, co-created by those in relationship? And the elder asked, "What *brings forth* that rainbow?" Taking it deeper, at each juncture of the research and writing, I needed to acknowledge, deconstruct and adjust my own white, male privilege, my own colonizing predications, and challenge the same in the environments within which I traveled. Could I critically self-reflect, and critique the academy? Could I get off the security of my old wooden bench? Could I be as a child wrapped in the cradleboard of my host, and truly listen and feel with my heart?

And then, "how would I begin to convey *hnkhwelkhwlnet* to others?" The challenges continue. Early on I appreciated the unequivocal relationship between *what* I was researching, i.e., relating to orality-based narratives and behaviors—*how* that content was conveyed, i.e., acts of verbal and symbolic discourse, such as storytelling and ritual procedures—and *who* were the "others," i.e., the recipients of the storytelling. If I was to begin to convey *hnkhwelkhwlnet* content, applying my best word-sculping skills, I needed to attempt to use an appropriate means, aligning the *how* with the *what*. And as with a good storyteller,

I needed to know my audience, rendering the story accessible without impairing its authenticity. To do otherwise would only distort what I sought to convey, "whitewash the Indigenous."

Here comes the rub. How would I and my co-authors publish through a media, e.g., professional journal or book manuscript, that in its literacy-based nature could undermine the orality-based message we wished to convey? In seeking a better alignment, the means we'd use needed to come closer to acts of traditional storytelling, of *baaéechichiwaau* (Apsáalooke) and *'me'y'mi'y'm* (Schitsu'umsh). To help provide an oral nuance and sense of the rhythm in the telling, when opting for a written media, we transcribed narratives using a poetic style, complete with intonation, pause and hand gesture markings. We even encouraged the reader to first access the story through the voice of someone reading to him or her, to better experience the orality of the unfolding story. We've also "published" via the web, on internet modules that streamed elders being interviewed and retelling stories, providing a more authentic auditory and visual experience. And most recently, we've found an intriguing alignment in the application of orality-based content through an interactive 3D virtual reality web module. The "user" becomes an avatar, interacting via a joystick with an elder, as a traditional root is gathered. If not "listening" to the elder's dialogue and responding to his subtle directions, the story ceases and the module must be initiated anew. In the experience, the user is offered implicitly conveyed Indigenous teachings. Surprisingly, this cutting-edge media technology has parallels with the structures and dynamics of Indigenous orality-based storytelling. Regardless of format, publishing comes with financial costs, often contingent on marketability, a benefactor or grantsmanship. Ultimately, there cannot be a substitute for the experience of engaging directly with an elder's storytelling. But in our ethnographic endeavors seeking a wider audience, can we at least better appreciate the challenges and begin to address them? Can engaging a book begin to create an experience conveying placed-based teachings through the transitory intersection of the elder with the Coyote with you, the reader?

"What are you *gonna do* with what you've learned?" Fundamental to the Indigenous way is sharing with those in need, to give back to others. In our anthropological history, there's been too much taking. The "give back" certainly needs to be defined by the community. I've been involved in a range of applied projects, addressing such issues as health care delivery, a language arts curriculum, a natural resource damage assessment, climate change, and an Indigenous perspective on Lewis and Clark. Stories that seek to make a difference.

Does not successful ethnographic publishing really start with an invite and permission, moves to collaboration and relationship, adding a dose of deep self-reflection along with some suspension of disbelief, a dash of aligning the *how* with the *what* with the *who*, culminating in giving back? With challenges faced at each juncture of the journey. Can publication be other than the offspring of a labor of love, and certainly not the impetus for the research? While there are other routes to publishing, I suspect if you've successfully traveled the "tin shed," you could be well along your way to publishing.

I *baaéechichiwaau*, aka, write, to re-tell the cherished stories that celebrate diversity and reveal the ubiquitous, in the hope of making a difference. I've found no greater satisfaction than in the act of re-telling the stories, be they in oral or written form. Late into the evening, after sharing his favorite stories, to be included in an anthology we were putting together, the elder turned to me and affirmed, "If all these *great* stories were told...great stories *will come!*"

Ahókaash to all my teachers, co-researchers and co-authors. To the reader, may this story bring you a difference.

You can glimpse my publication history at: http://www.webpages.uidaho.edu/~rfrey/

Conclusion

Writing and Publishing in Anthropology: Voices, Insights, and Disciplinary Trends

Tiffany J. Fulkerson and Shannon Tushingham

We appreciate Darby Stapp and Julie Longenecker flipping the typical organization of contributed volume compilations—here, we (the most junior authors of all the participants) have been given the position of commenting on essays by a group of prolific and influential senior writers. This is in keeping with the intent of this endeavor: as stated in the introduction, the purpose of this special section is to encourage and inspire other professionals to write and publish. The call was met with an enthusiastic and impressive response. In in just two months, nineteen writers sent in their essays, with commentary ranging from practical tips on how to write, to views on research ethics and the struggles of publishing. The essays are not only entertaining and often deeply candid, but also the individual stories offer profound insight into the reasons why these individuals write. While much of the imparted wisdom is directed at early career professionals, this effort is also aimed at encouraging mid-career and senior authors to share their wisdom and life's work for the purposes of posterity and ushering valuable hidden knowledge into the light.

Accounts such as these are important, not just because they are inspirational, but also because they can provide insight into larger disciplinary patterns. Understanding how and why people write is central to our research, which examines trends in the production and dissemination of knowledge in North American archaeology. We are specifically concerned with who dominates discourses in STEM sciences and the systemic factors that influence individual decisions to write, while advocating for multivocality and equity. We have compiled large-scale datasets that demonstrate that women, cultural resource management (CRM), and agency archaeologists publish significantly less than men and academics in peer-reviewed journals. The reasons for these inequities are many and include the simple cost-benefit dynamics of publishing, which vary according to one's occupation, gender, and other intersectional identities (e.g., Tushingham et al. 2017; Fulkerson and Tushingham 2019). We believe that promoting multivocality will provide many benefits to our discipline, and by shedding light on these dynamics and addressing some of the systemic issues, it is possible to promote a broader range of perspectives and voices in archaeology discourse.

Writing can be hard, lonely business, as is navigating the peer-review process. This set of essays provides a great deal of insight into the detailed mechanics of writing, as well as writing philosophies, motivations, and approaches. Below, we review some of the major themes that are covered. For the seasoned scholar, writing may come as second nature, but it goes without saying that such knowledge is not magically imparted on writers (except, perhaps, for a few charmed individuals), and without proper mentorship, it can often be very difficult for young writers to break into and establish a career in writing. It is also important for mentors, editors, and senior scholars to acknowledge that young anthropologists face a very different professional and publishing landscape than they were once socialized into, and so we conclude our essay with commentary about the changing landscape of writing and publishing and some thoughts on how individual writers may navigate this brave new world.

Reviewing the Essays: Sampling Considerations

The nineteen contributing authors in this compilation of essays encompass a variety of occupations in anthropology (see Stapp and Longenecker, introduction to this collection), which affords a diversity of professional perspectives. It bears noting, however, that only four of the nineteen authors are women, which amounts to 21% of participants. This, of course, is not representative of the high proportion of women anthropologists working in the northwest today, but it is consistent with observations made by some of the few women authors who contributed to this special section (see below). It also parallels research findings demonstrating that women remain inadequately represented in anthropology publishing. For example, Bardolph (2014:527) found that women comprised only 29% of first/single authors in regional publication venues in North American archaeology from 1990–2013, while our own research demonstrates that women accounted for a mere 27% of first/single authors in peer-reviewed journals from western North America from 2000–2018 (Fulkerson and Tushingham 2019).

The disproportion of women to men authors in this special section was not an intentional editorial slight—Stapp initially contacted those former *JONA* authors and peer reviewers who he knew published a lot or cared about writing. Of the original invitees, eight (32%) were women (Darby Stapp, personal communication). Not all who were given the opportunity chose to or could participate. While the intentions were not to obtain a representative sample of people who write in anthropology, the demographic makeup of the nineteen authors who ultimately participated mirror other trends in anthropology beyond men/women ratios. North American anthropology has historically been and continues to be dominated by white, heteronormative, and cisgender people, and there is a strong male bias among older generations of practitioners (e.g., see Zeder 1994). As Stapp and Longenecker noted in the introduction to this special section, 100% of the contributing authors are white, while the average age of the authors is approximately 65. Thus, the demographic makeup of the contributing authors is illustrative of some of the complex historical and idiosyncratic factors that can factor into issues surrounding publication and demography. Future essay compilations may garner insights from Indigenous people/People of Color and LGBTQ+ individuals, which would not only help to clarify the dynamics of writing and publishing for these underrepresented groups, but would also help to illuminate why such people are not well represented among practitioners and those who publish in the discipline. Future research and solicited insights from people with identities that are underrepresented or have been historically marginalized, as well as from younger authors and even non-anthropologists, will help to provide a more inclusive understanding of writing and publishing in northwest anthropology.

Essay Insights on Writing and Publishing. The essays cover several themes: 1) writing philosophies, approaches, and insights; 2) challenges of writing and publishing; 3) motivations and rewards of writing and publishing; and 4) advice and recommendation for students and colleagues. In some cases, writing philosophies/approaches and advice were implied rather than explicit, being illuminated through anecdotal experiences. Often, they were closely tied to or indiscernible from one another. While challenging, we made a good faith effort to summarize some of the key insights from the nineteen papers with careful consideration of the messages conveyed by the contributing authors.

Writing Philosophies, Approaches, and Insights. A recurrent theme in the compilation of essays is that of change. Carlson, J. Miller, Mierendorf, and others observed that technological advancements have precipitated considerable change in the world of writing and publishing. Online access to journals and other internet resources have provided new solutions to knowledge dissemination and can influence decisions of where and how to publish. As noted by Carlson, the digital revolution has or may be rendering some print journals obsolete as online methods of research communication change the cost and speed of publication.

Many essays emphasized the importance of writing well. Becoming a good writer requires time, dedication, and training. It often necessitates the development of an effective writing style. Several papers criticized common approaches to writing that employ excessive jargon that isn't accessible to a wider audience. Numerous authors noted the importance of writing clearly and concisely. Several stressed the utility of committing to a writing schedule and reading widely, both within and outside of anthropology. Adherence to these approaches affords developing writers the opportunity to find their voice, which Warner and B. Miller reminded incipient authors to put time and effort into developing.

A number of essays emphasized the need to consider the impact of research and writing on the many stakeholders of anthropology. Anthropology is a collaborative enterprise that includes multiple participatory and invested communities, from Indigenous groups and the general public to agencies and clients. Blukis Onat, Frey, Reynolds, Kehoe, Mierendorf, and Dauble pointed out the need for writing that reaches Indigenous communities and the public, as well as writing that incorporates Indigenous perspectives. While anthropologists are (or should be) well aware of the past and even present transgressions of our discipline, we see from these essays that decolonized and intersectional approaches to writing may serve to mend grievances and build cultural bridges moving forward.

Insights into gender disparities and patriarchal systems that continue to limit the participation of women in publishing come from Kehoe and Moss. Kehoe reminded us that women are less likely to publish when they, as people, are overlooked by society. Moss provided anecdotal experiences to highlight gendered dimensions of writing and publishing that often disadvantage women. Consistent with our own research and the research of others (e.g., Bardolph 2014; Tushingham et al. 2017; Fulkerson and Tushingham 2019), Moss and Kehoe spoke to the underrepresentation of women in publishing and the underappreciation of women's writing, especially within the realms of theory.

While there was a wide diversity of writing philosophies and approaches that materialized throughout the nineteen essays, it is clear that persistence is a shared quality of the prolific writers who contributed to this special section. Lyman, Croes, and J. Miller highlighted the importance of persistence when pursuing publication. Indeed, it is fair to assume that nearly every writer who has gone through the painstaking process of publishing their work has been faced with the challenges of putting "pen to paper" (or rather, "fingers to keyboard"), tackling the drudgery of editing, and maneuvering through obstacles set forth by reviewers, committee members, and editors. As it were, a recurrent theme throughout the compilation of papers has been the modern-day challenges of writing and publishing—challenges which, no doubt, account for much of the contemporary lack of writing output that several authors observed.

Challenges of Writing and Publishing. In the frank words of Butler, "Writing is hard." Many authors observed that the writing and publishing process is time and energy consuming. Personal limitations include fear of ridicule, lack of drive or commitment, perfectionism, and life in general. Then there are the systemic and institutional barriers to publishing that our aforementioned research addresses. Anthropologists are employed in a wide variety of professions including academia and CRM, the latter of which comprises 90% of archaeologists in the U.S. (Sebastian 2009:7). King, Griffin, Plew, Carlson, Moss, Kehoe, Warner, and Ames spoke to changes in the professional landscape of anthropology that have complicated publishing in modernity. These difficulties include but are not limited to: fewer tenure-track positions and lack of proper mentorship in academia, lack of incentives and support for publishing for those in CRM, the necessity of time-consuming emails, and the increasing emphasis on high-impact journals, which has reduced incentives to produce monographs and publish in regional venues (see also our discussion below).

<u>Motivations and Rewards to Write and Publish.</u> Regardless of the many challenges, there is a resounding consensus among the authors that writing and publishing can be deeply satisfying and rewarding. Many of the prolific writers indicated that they enjoy communicating their research and collaborating with colleagues. Lyman, Plew, and Dauble observed that writing and publishing make us better thinkers and teachers. As Kehoe noted, it allows us to have our voices heard. Authors share a desire to contribute to and shape their field, as Ames pointed out. Butler indicated that writing helps to build a sense of community and ensure posterity, while Butler and J. Miller discussed the delayed gratification of seeing a project through to completion. For those who work closely with Indigenous and host communities, satisfaction can come from Indigenous collaboration and conveying knowledge through Native perspective, as detailed by Frey, Blukis Onat, and Croes. Importantly, numerous authors reminded us that anthropologists have a professional obligation to disseminate their work. We maintain an ethical obligation to communicate the results of our studies not only to each other, but also to the public and the communities that we write about.

<u>Advice and Recommendations.</u> The contributing authors of this issue imparted invaluable advice about research, writing, editing, and publishing that students, junior colleagues, and even seasoned authors will undoubtedly benefit from embracing. We briefly reference or directly quote some of their wisdom as follows:

- Read a lot and widely (Butler, King).
- Recognize the value of your research. Gain confidence and lose your inhibitions and biases (Griffin, Warner, B. Miller, Frey).

- Make your data and fieldwork results available (Carlson, Croes).
- Do not wait for inspiration to write. Just do it (Butler, King).
- Commit to writing copiously and consistently (Butler, Lyons, Mierendorf, King).
- Find your audience and know them (Croes, Dauble, Frey, Mierendorf).
- "When in doubt, cut it out" (Ames).
- "Kill your babies" (Ames).
- "Eschew BS" (King).
- All first drafts "are crap" (Lyons).
- "...'done' is always better than perfect" (Lyons).
- "Epic performance is the result of epic preparation" (Lyons).
- Don't edit while you write. The editing and revision processes are essential components of writing (Ames, Butler, Kehoe, Lyons).
- Learn and improve from reviewer feedback (Lyman).
- Build a thick skin when it comes to the peer-review process (Lyman).
- Writers: support publishers. Editors: be more proactive (Mierendorf, Plew).
- Encourage more compliance archaeologists to publish. Challenge non-disclosure provisions in CRM contracts that inhibit publication. Use publication as a form of mitigation (Plew, Griffin).
- Share with and give back to the descendant and host communities that you research or collaborate with (Blukis Onat, Frey, Reynolds).

The Present and Future of Knowledge Production and Dissemination for Anthropologists in the Pacific Northwest (and Elsewhere)

<u>The Changing Landscape of Writing and Publishing</u>. Stapp and Longenecker presented a basic question to the authors: "Why don't we write more?" The answer is not straightforward. We contend that people write a lot—the volume of written output has grown exponentially, particularly if one

counts technical report writing, which has exploded after the growth of CRM. We have found that extra-academic professionals publish more in non-peer-reviewed venues than peer-reviewed ones (e.g., Tushingham et al. 2017; Fulkerson and Tushingham 2019), and it is for this reason that we have suggested that such an outlet, if introduced, might benefit dissemination of knowledge in the northwest region (Fulkerson and Tushingham 2018). The landscape of publishing is different for academic professionals, where pressures to publish remain constant and have even heightened. Publication output for academics is especially important in today's job market, where coveted tenure-track faculty positions are becoming increasingly scarce (Speakman et al. 2018; see also Ames, this volume). Taken together, it seems that people are still writing and publishing in high numbers. So how do we explain the lack of writing output that was observed by the contributors to this special section? As some of the contributing authors have hinted at or suggested, we believe that what we are seeing is a trend towards reduced writing and manuscript submissions among specific research dissemination outlets, which, at least in part, is a response to changes in technology and the standards for measuring professional success in modernity.

Impact Factors, Online Dissemination, and Today's Hyper-Competitive Academic Market. There has been an accelerated push in academia to embrace quantitative metrics as a measure of productivity and research impact. Such measurements include the Journal Impact Factor score, the h-factor, and altmetrics. These measurements consider both the quantity and presumed quality of papers. Consequently, peer-reviewed papers, especially those with higher impact scores (which tend to be national/international in scope), typically hold greater weight in academia (see Moss, this collection). In general, those with higher frequencies of influential publications are more likely to be selected for tenure-track jobs and to secure tenure once they have obtained a faculty position (see Griffin, this collection). Students also feel these pressures—at least those who seek academic faculty positions. In today's hyper-competitive academic job market, candidates with a low number of publications will have a tough time getting a job, much less an interview.

    The hyper-competitive job market and emphasis on publication output influences decisions of where and what to publish, while encouraging a new world of active dissemination. In the age of digital open access publications, altmetrics (a measure of public impact as measured by online news stories, Twitter, Facebook, blogs, and other social media outlets, etc.), and for-profit repositories that allow researchers to make their works available online for free (Academia.edu, ResearchGate, etc.), researchers are navigating new territories that allow them to actively publicize their work in unprecedented and more highly visible ways.

All of these variables have both positive and negative effects on publishing. On the one hand, this phenomenon can be beneficial as it pushes individuals to circulate their work and provides more opportunities to communicate research than ever before. On the other, it encourages many writers to focus on "high impact" journals at the detriment of regional and "low impact" ones. Importantly, papers in journals that afford high impact scores do not necessarily equate to high *quality* papers. Indeed, some of the most valuable works that we're familiar with come from technical reports, theses/dissertations, monographs, and regional journals like *JONA*—all of which typically either garner low impact factor scores or are not rated at all by the modern quantitative metrics reviewed above. Today, writers may opt to "salami slice" their research, cut corners, or engage in other behaviors that will strengthen their publication output, even at the expense of research and writing quality. While we don't agree with all of these practices, it's critical to understand the current dynamics of writing and publishing and the pressures and constraints that young scholars face, and to acknowledge that this is a very different landscape than older generations of writers grew up in.

<u>The Growth of Extra-Academic Anthropology.</u> It is important to acknowledge that conversations about writing and publishing typically revolve around academic publishing, yet only a small proportion of anthropologists are in academia, and an even smaller number are in research-intensive universities. In archaeology, as with many other fields, there has been a major growth in the private sector and in agency work since the mid-1970s. Key regulatory developments led to the expansion of "compliance archaeology," which involves Section 106 and related management activities conducted by government agencies and CRM outfits. Those who work in this field produce a great deal of written

work—technical reports, National Register of Historic Places nominations, etc. While some of the best archaeology work is done by compliance professionals, too often this research is not widely disseminated, and thus remains hidden from much of the archaeology community, let alone the public (Lipe 2009:50). Although individuals in non-academic anthropology professions may produce the greatest volume of written work, academic anthropologists continue to publish a great deal more in both regional and national peer-reviewed journals. Realistically, it can be a challenge for CRM and other professionals to find the time to write up their results in venues such as *JONA*, but finding ways to facilitate and encourage such submissions would only serve to benefit the discipline (see also King, Griffin, Carlson, Ames, this collection).

<u>The Future of Knowledge Production and Dissemination.</u> While it is difficult to predict the future of anthropological writing and publishing, evaluating past and current trends in the discipline provides insights into potential future directions. For most of us, writing is and will continue to be a non-negotiable skill. Anthropologists and early career professionals must learn to write, write a lot, and write well. They must also navigate a new landscape of publishing, with both opportunities and constraints that are quite different from earlier generations. Successfully maneuvering through the formidable publishing landscapes of today and the future will require individual persistence and the ability to adapt to the many obstacles that will invariably be encountered.

In order to maintain the relevance of anthropology as a discipline, and out of obligation to the stakeholders that frequently fund or contribute to anthropology projects, it is critical that we become more proactive about conveying our research and its importance to each other, the communities that we study, and the public. This will require strengthening collaboration efforts, supporting regional journals that allow us to communicate research to our colleagues in visible ways, and using online resources as well as digital media and non-traditional communication forums in order to disseminate research through new, ethical, and innovative approaches.

There remains a persistent gap in the visibility of the work of certain groups in anthropology, which inhibits the diversity of voices and perspectives that contribute to and shape our field. Today, roughly half or more of anthropologists are women, and most work in extra-academic settings. If the current market share and hiring environments are any indication (see Speakman et al. 2018), these trends are likely to continue or grow. Moving forward, we should cultivate an environment that encourages the voices of not only women and non-academics, but importantly, Indigenous people/People of Color, LGBTQ+ groups, and other periphery groups that remain underrepresented in publishing. Ensuring a more robust and equitable future for anthropology writing and publishing will necessitate strong mentorship, support for CRM and agency professionals to publish their work in accessible forums, the dissolution of institutional impediments to publishing for certain demographics, individual persistence and perseverance, and certainly not least, taking to heart the invaluable wisdom that the contributors to this special section graciously imparted.

REFERENCES CITED

Bardolph, Dana N.
2014   A Critical Evaluation of Recent Gendered Publishing Trends in American Archaeology. *American Antiquity,* 79(3):522–540.

Fulkerson, Tiffany J., and Shannon Tushingham
2018   Equity, Multivocality, and the Need for a Non-Peer-Reviewed Journal for Pacific Northwest Archaeology. *Association for Washington Archaeology Newsletter,* 22(3):9–11.

2019   Who Dominates the Discourses of the Past? Gender, Occupational Affiliation, and Multivocality in North American Archaeology Publishing. *American Antiquity.* Accepted for publication pending minor revisions.

Lipe, William D.
2009   Archaeological Values and Resource Management. In *Archaeology & Cultural Resource Management: Visions for the Future,* edited by Lynne Sebastian and William D. Lipe, pp. 41–64. Santa Fe, NM: School for Advanced Research Press.

Sebastian, Lynne
2009   The Future of CRM Archaeology. In *Archaeology & Cultural Resource Management: Visions for the Future,* edited by Lynne Sebastian and William D. Lipe, pp. 3–18. Santa Fe, NM: School for Advanced Research Press.

Speakman, Robert J., Carla S. Hadden, Matthew H. Colvin, Justin Cramb, K. C. Jones, Travis W. Jones, Isabelle Lulewicz, Katharine G. Napora, Katherine L. Reinberger, Brandon T. Ritchison, Alexandra R. Edwards, and Victor D. Thompson
2018   Market Share and Recent Hiring Trends in Anthropology Faculty Positions. *PLoS ONE,* 13(9):e0202528.

Tushingham, Shannon, Tiffany J. Fulkerson, and Katheryn Hill
2017   The Peer Review Gap: A Longitudinal Case Study of Gendered Publishing and Occupational Patterns in a Female-Rich Discipline, Western North America (1974–2016). *PLoS ONE,* 12(11):e0188403.

Zeder, Melinda A.
1997   *The American Archaeologist: A Profile.* Walnut Creek, CA: AltaMira.

ABOUT THE EDITORS

Darby C. Stapp (B.A., University of Denver; M.A., University of Idaho; Ph.D., University of Pennsylvania) and **Julia G. Longenecker** (B.A., University of Wyoming; M.A., University of Idaho) began their archaeological careers during the 1970s in the Rocky Mountain region of North America. After finishing their M.A. degrees at the University of Idaho, they moved to the Philadelphia area so that Darby could pursue his Ph.D. in historic archaeology from the University of Pennsylvania.

For the last 30 years, they have been working for various CRM Programs in the Northwest, specifically in the Columbia River Basin. For 20 years, Darby was the Cultural Resources Program Manager for Pacific Northwest National Laboratory (PNNL) at the Hanford site in southwestern Washington before retiring to form his own CRM firm, Northwest Anthropology LLC. Much of his work involves assisting local Tribes and the Wanapum to protect and preserve areas of cultural significance. He has served as Co-editor of the *Journal of Northwest Anthropology* since 2009.

Julie spent much of her career working for the Confederated Tribes of the Umatilla Indian Reservation (CTUIR), Cultural Resources Protection Program (CRPP), primarily assisting with cultural resource assessments and inadvertent discoveries of human remains. Since retiring from the Tribe in 2017, she has been able to assist Darby and Northwest Anthropology LLC with publishing and distributing the *Journal of Northwest Anthropology (JONA)*.

Stapp and Longenecker have published several articles together concerning the Kennewick Man, working with Tribes, and cultural resource management; and one book, *Avoiding Archaeological Disasters: A Risk Management Approach* (2009; Left Coast Press, Inc.).

darby.stapp@northwestanthropology.com
julie.longenecker@northwestanthropology.com

Tiffany J. Fulkerson is a Ph.D. candidate in the Department of Anthropology at WSU and a Field Archaeologist for Plateau Archaeological Investigations, LLC. She received her B.A. in Anthropology from Eastern Washington University (2009) and her M.A. in Interdisciplinary Studies (Anthropology and History) from Eastern Washington University (2012). She is an archaeologist whose interests include equity issues in archaeological practice and human responses to environmental and climatic changes in the precontact past. Her current research includes a reexamination of archaeological burial practices using decolonized and feminist approaches, along with examinations of longitudinal trends in the gender and occupational affiliation of archaeologists in various realms of disciplinary participation.

tiffany.fulkerson@wsu.edu

Shannon Tushingham is an Assistant Professor at the WSU Department of Anthropology and the Director of the WSU Museum of Anthropology. She received her B.A. in Anthropology from the University of Connecticut (1991), her M.S. in Public Archaeology from the University of Memphis (2000), and her Ph.D. from UC Davis (2009). She is an anthropological archaeologist with research broadly centered on human-environmental relationships and the archaeology of hunter-gatherer-fishers in western North America. She is a proponent of both field and legacy collections-based research and collaborative studies with Indigenous communities. Current research explores the historical ecology and evolution socio-economic systems in the northwest, as well as studies directed at understanding psychoactive plant use by worldwide human cultures.

shannon.tushingham@wsu.edu

Kenneth Ames
6116 SE Stephens Street
Portland, OR 97215
amesk@pdx.edu

Astrida R. Blukis Onat
boasinc@comcast.net

Virginia L. Butler
Department of Anthropology
Portland State University
Portland, OR 97207
virginia@pdx.edu

Roy Carlson
royc@sfu.ca

Dale R. Croes
dcroes444@gmail.com

Dennis Dauble
dennisdauble@icloud.com

Rodney Frey
208-885-6268
rfrey@uidaho.edu
https://www.webpages.uidaho.edu/~rfrey/
University of Idaho Dept. Sociology/Anthropology 875 Perimeter Dr. MS 1110
Moscow, Idaho 83844-1110

Dennis Griffin
Oregon State Historic Preservation Office
725 Summer St. SE
Salem, Oregon 97301
Dennis.Griffin@oregon.gov

Alice B. Kehoe
3014 N. Shepard Ave., Milwaukee WI
53211-3436
akehoe@uwm.edu

Tom F. King
tomking106@gmail.com

R. Lee Lyman
Department of Anthropology
112 Swallow Hall, University of Missouri
Columbia, MO 65211
lymanr@missouri.edu

Kevin J. Lyons
kjlyons@kalispeltribe.com

Robert R. Mierendorf
rrmcascades@gmail.com

Bruce Granville Miller
Professor, Department of Anthropology,
Canadian Anthropology Society Fellow
University of British Columbia
6303 NW Marine Dr
Vancouver, BC V6T 1Z1
604-822-6336

Jay Miller
jaymiller4@juno.com

Madonna L. Moss
mmoss@uoregon.edu

Mark G. Plew
University Distinguished Professor
Department of Anthropology, Boise State University
1910 University Drive
Boise, Idaho 83725
mplew@boisestate.edu

Nathan Reynolds
Cowlitz Indian Tribe; P.O. Box 2547
Longview, WA 98632
nreynolds@cowlitz.org

Mark S. Warner
mwarner@uidaho.edu

Made in the
USA
Middletown, DE